Mediterranean Instant Pot Cookbook

Easy, and Healthy Mediterranean Diet Instant Pot Recipes for Busy People. Lose Your Weight Fast with Amazing Recipes for Your Electric Pressure Cooker

Author: Linda Holman

CONTENTS

Introduction 6

The History Of The Mediterranean Diet 6

Why The Mediterranean Diet? 7

Studies On The Mediterranean Diet 7

Mediterranean Diet Rules 9

Foods You Can Eat 9

Foods To Avoid 10

Things You Should Know About Your Instant Pot 10

Differences Between Electric And Stove-Top Pressure Cookers 12

Health Benefits Of Pressure Cooking 13

Poultry Recipes 16

1 - Family Dinner Chicken 16

2 - Popular Chicken Cacciatore 17

3 - Famous Chicken Piccata 18

4 - Flavorsome Caprese Chicken 19

5 - Purely Greek Flavored Chicken 20

6 - Braised Chicken 21

7 - Moroccan Chicken Meal 22

8 - Saucy Chicken 23

9 - Healthier Chicken Dinner 24

10 - Inspiring Chicken Drumsticks 25

11 - Balanced Spicy Chicken 26

12 - Drunken Chicken & Mushrooms 27

13 - Creamy Chicken Breasts 28

14 - 2-Cheeses Chicken 29

15 - Low-Carb Dinner Meal 30

16 - Souvlaki Inspired Chicken Bowl 31

17 - Protein-Packed Bowl 32

18 - Colorful Chicken & Rice Platter 33

19 - Tuscan Chicken Rice 34

20 - Favorite Italian Chicken Pasta 35

Red Meat Recipes 36

21 - Flavorful Chuck Shoulder 36

22 - Yummy Chuck Roast 37

23 - Nourishing Dinner Beef 38

24 - Italian Zesty Beef 39

25 - Family Friendly Meatballs Spaghetti 40

26 - Lombard Osso Buco 41

27 - Favorite Greek Dinner 42

28 - Aromatic Leg of Lamb 43

29 - Garlicky Lamb Shoulder 44

30 - Spice Marinated Lamb Shanks 45

31 - Succulent Lamb Shanks 46

32 - Tomato Braised Lamb Shanks 47

33 - Greek Flavoring Meatballs 48

34 - Abruzzi Style Lamb Pasta 49

35 - Weekend Dinner Pork Roast 50

38 - Herbed Pork Shoulder 51

36 - Glazed Pork Tenderloin 52

37 - Intense Flavored Pork Chops 53

39 - Delicious Weeknight Meal 54

40 - Ultra Creamy Pork Ragu 55

Fish & Seafood Recipes 56

41 - Simplest Frozen Salmon 56

42 - Omega-3 Rich Salmon 57

43 - Welcoming Salmon Dinner 58

44 - Flavor-Packed Cod 59

45 - One-Pot Dinner Cod 60

46 - Terrific Protein Dinner 61

47 - Robust Fish Meal 62

48 - Southern Italian Tuna Pasta 63

49 - High-Protein Shrimp Meal 64

50 - Fancy Shrimp Scampi 65

51 - Rustic Shrimp Risotto 66

52 - Richly Creamy Shrimp Spaghetti 67

53 - Amazing Shrimp Pasta 68

54 - Mussels 69

55 - Super-Simple Octopus 70

Vegetarian & Vegan Recipes 71

56 - Spring Side Dish 71

57 - High-Carb Luncheon 72

58 - 3-Veggies Combo 73

59 - Winner Stuffed Acorn Squash 74

60 - Savory Herbed Quinoa 75

61 - Bold Flavors Loaded Meal 76

62 - Plant-Based Dinner 77

63 - Vegan-Friendly Bolognese 78

64 - Summery Luncheon Chickpeas 79

65 - Uniquely Tasty Beans 80

66 - Green Garden Risotto 81

67 - Italian Style Mac n' Cheese 82

68 - Light Pasta Meal 83

69 - Best-Ever Hummus 84

70 - Cheese-Free Queso 85

Soups & Stews Recipes 86

71 - Immunity Boosting Chicken Soup 86

72 - Classic Wedding Soup 87

73 - Hearty Pasta e Fagioli Soup 88

74 - Rustic Tortellini Soup 89

75 - Effortless Veggie Soup 90

76 - Bright Green Soup 91

77 - Exciting Chickpeas Soup 92

78 - Comfort Food Soup 93

79 - Turkish Lentil Soup 94

80 - Satisfying Vegan Soup 95

81 - Cozy Night Chicken Stew 96

82 - Sweet & Savory Stew 97

83 - Wednesday Night Dinner Stew 98

84 - Comfy Meal Stew 99

85 - Toe-Warming Lamb Stew 100

86 - Fragrant Fish Stew 101

87 - Winter Dinner Stew 102

88 - Palestinian Okra Stew 103

89 - Meatless-Monday Chickpeas Stew 104

90 - Super-Quick Stew 105

Dessert Recipes 106

91 - Berry Season Compote 106

92 - Elegant Dessert Pears 107

93 - Apple Juice Poached Pears 108

94 - Chocolate Lover's Cake 109

95 - Moist Date Cake 110

96 - Delicious Coffee-Time Cake 111

97 - Delightful Cream Cake 112

98 - Zesty Cheesecake 113

99 - Greek Wedding Cheesecake 114

100 - Sweet-Tooth Carving Tiramisu Cheesecake 115

Conclusion 116

INTRODUCTION

The Mediterranean diet has become quite a popular option for people who want to enjoy the benefits that come with plant-based foods today. The diet has gained attention from scientific experts and researchers from all regions of the world. Many studies have already been conducted to understand the benefits that may come with a Mediterranean diet.

People who follow a Mediterranean diet have been found to have a lower risk of heart disease, inflammation, and reduced body weight. Blood sugar is also seemingly regulated by following this type of diet.

Preparation of meals that are suitable for a Mediterranean diet can sometimes take some time. This is why it is not uncommon to see people who follow this particular diet use an instant pot or pressure cooker. These devices make preparing meals much faster and easier. At the same time, they also provide added benefits when following a Mediterranean diet.

In this post, we look at what the Mediterranean diet is. We also take a brief look at the history of the diet. The post considers the many health benefits that have been associated with the diet. Additionally, we also look at the benefits that may come with using a pressure cooker or instant pot to prepare meals while following the Mediterranean diet.

The History Of The Mediterranean Diet

The Mediterranean diet is based on eating habits from multiple cultures. The diet was initially published by a husband and wife team. Biologist Ancel Keys and Markaret Keys, a chemist, worked together in order to develop a diet that focuses on providing a combination of different eating habits into one diet. It was first made public in 1975.

The diet essentially takes from eating habits related to Italy and Greece. The eating habits contained within the Mediterranean diet were very popular in these two countries within the 1960s.

During the early stages, after the diet was made public, it failed to gain much attention. In the 1990s, however, the diet quickly gained recognition. People quickly started to adopt the diet, particularly due to the health claims made by the authors.

Researchers took note of the Mediterranean diet and started to conduct studies. These studies quickly made the world aware of the health benefits that may come with the eating habits introduced by Ancel Keys and Markaret Keys.

Why The Mediterranean Diet?

The Mediterranean diet focuses on teaching us how to intake more fresh vegetables and fruits in our diet and with that introducing all the vital vitamins and minerals that our body requires. And while you are supposed to eat red meat on only rare occasions, fish and seafood are a must. Eggs, yogurt, milk, and cheese are also welcomed but in moderation. Sweets, artificial sweeteners, processed meat, and highly processed foods have no place in the Mediterranean diet.

The Mediterranean diet has been reported to have many health benefits.

- Improved cardiovascular health
- Reduced risk of health disease and heart attack
- Low cholesterol levels
- Reduced risk of hypertension
- Reduced risk of stroke
- Reduced risk of diabetes mellitus and improved condition among those with diabetes mellitus
- Weight loss
- Reduced facial wrinkles, dark spots on the skin

Studies On The Mediterranean Diet

A large number of scientific studies have been conducted on the Mediterranean diet to date. Many of these studies had shown positive effects when the diet was adopted by people with certain diseases. Additionally, the diet is also a great choice for promoting general health. People who follow a Mediterranean diet seem to complain less about certain diseases and disorders.

To provide a better view of the benefits that the diet may offer, we need to turn our focus toward studies published on the topic.

A large study involved a total of 7,447 participants. The published paper was termed the "PREDIMED Study." All of the individuals who took part in the study had high-risk factors linked to heart disease. Three diets were used among the participants. This was also a long-term study, lasting for a period of five years.

A control group was introduced, who was offered a low-fat diet. The other two groups both consumed meals that were in line with the Mediterranean diet. The one group was instructed to follow a Mediterranean diet with extra virgin olive oil, while the other group followed the diet with additional nuts added.

The study was divided into multiple sections. Various results were obtained, but the majority of findings pointed toward positive effects related to the Mediterranean diet.

There was a 31% reduction in the risk of heart disease in the group who consumed a Mediterranean diet with extra virgin olive oil. Among those with extra nuts, a 28% reduction in the risk for death from heart-related events were noted. Similar results were not noted among the participants part of the control group.

In one study, it was shown that the Mediterranean diet provided effective results within as short of a period as three months. There was a reduction in various cardiovascular risk factors noted when participants were provided this diet for a 90-day period.

Improvements were found in the following vitals and measurements:

- Blood sugar levels
- Systolic blood pressure levels
- Total cholesterol and cholesterol ratio
- C-reactive protein levels

In another study, it was shown that the Mediterranean diet might also be highly effective at helping a person with weight management. Total cholesterol, weight, and endothelial function score were recorded among participants.

Among those who followed a Mediterranean diet, there was an average reduction of 8.8 pounds in body weight. Among those who were part of a low-fat control group, the average weight reduction was recorded as 2.6 pounds.

The Mediterranean diet also provided a significant improvement in Endothelial function among the participants. Such an improvement was not noted among the people who were part of a control group.

In addition to these findings, researchers also noted a reduction in insulin resistance markings. Inflammatory markers among the participants who followed a Mediterranean diet were also reduced.

Mediterranean Diet Rules

To experience the health benefits associated with the Mediterranean diet, it is important for a person to understand the rules that come with this eating style. The diet is not very strict, but there are a few important rules to comply with. By following through with all these rules, there is a greater chance of experiencing the benefits that scientific studies have linked to a Mediterranean diet.

The primary rule of the Mediterranean diet is to adopt eating habits that prioritize plant-based foods instead of meat-based foods. The majority of foods that are included in the diet are of plant-based origin.

Even though plant-based foods are prioritized, it should be noted that it does not mean a person can never eat other foods. Some alternative foods are allowed in moderation or occasionally. Eating too much of the foods that should only be included occasionally can, however, reduce the benefits that the diet is able to offer a person.

Here is the basic structure of the Mediterranean diet:

- Foundation: Plant-based foods
- Moderate: Seafood, poultry, eggs, and dairy
- Occasionally: Red meat

Foods You Can Eat

There are a lot of foods that can be included in a Mediterranean diet - but you should make sure you do understand the specifics.

The main foods that are generally considered an important part of the diet include those that are processed from plant sources. Examples of these include:

- Vegetables and fruit (Up to 10 servings per day)
- Nuts
- Beans
- Whole grains
- Herbs
- Spices

These are the primary foods that meals are built around – additional foods in other categories can then be added at specific occasions.

Red wine can also be consumed, but only in moderation.

People who eat a lot of bread should make a few changes. When following a Mediterranean diet, white bread should be switched out for whole wheat bread. There are also whole grain options when looking at pasta and pizza dough. These are excellent alternatives.

Fruit juice can be consumed, but not in excess amounts. An unsweetened fruit juice still contains a lot of sugars. Sugar is something that is generally avoided as much as possible on a Mediterranean diet.

Foods To Avoid

While there are quite a few foods that can be included in a Mediterranean diet, people also need to be aware of what they should not include. There are many foods that can interfere with the diet's ability to offer the body the claimed benefits.

Some of the most important foods to avoid when following a Mediterranean diet include:

- Hot dogs
- Processed meat products
- Deli meat products
- Refined grains (white pasta, pizza dough made with white flour, and white bread)
- Food that contains a lot of added sugar (soda, candy, and pastries)
- Refined oils (Soybean oil and canola oil are examples)

Things You Should Know About Your Instant Pot

You just bought your very first instant pot? Or maybe you are still thinking about purchasing one? Being a beginner in this whole new way of cooking or thinking about dipping your toes in this water always comes with a dose of nervousness.

At this point, you don't know if pressure cooking is the right option for you or how you would handle it.

One thing you should know is that you don't really need some exceptional culinary skills to use a pressure cooker. This appliance is incredibly easy to use, and as you're using it more often, your experience and cooking skills will develop.

1. It is intuitive

What does this mean? If you've never used any type of pressure cooker before, it will take some time for you to get used to the new cooking style. At the same time, it's not complicated to learn everything about it.

2. Pressure-can, no, you can't!

Pressure sensor regulates pressure cooker, not a thermometer. As a result, the actual temperature might change depending on your location's elevation. Moreover, the USDA did not test the safety of Instant pot in pressure-canning.

On the other hand, you can do boiling-water canning, which is suitable for jams and pickles.

3. Instant pots are easy to clean

If you are tired of all those appliances that are difficult to clean, you will love your Instant pot.

The instant pot has a multitude of advantages, but one of the best things about it is a simple and easy cleaning process.

4. You'll have to convert 15 psi recipes

The reason for this is simple – pressure cookers operate at 15 psi, 250°F, (pounds per square inch) while the Instant pot functions at 11.6 psi or 242°F.

Therefore, when you come across recipes that recommend 15psi, the best thing to do is to cook a few minutes longer.

5. Sauté feature can do way more

Saute is just one of many features that come with your Instant Pot, and it's safe to say it will be one of your favorite options to use.

You can:

- Sauté vegetables before cooking a meal in order to soften them up and enhance the flavor of the dish

- Cook pasta, e.g., when you are about to prepare a soup which includes pasta.

- Thick sauces by mixing cornstarch with cold water and adding the mixture to a sauce in the pot. Then, turn on the sauté and wait for a few minutes.

Differences Between Electric And Stove-Top Pressure Cookers

Pressure cooking is highly practical, and it has become a popular cooking method. We can divide pressure cookers into electric and stove-top appliances.

While it is easy to assume these units are the same, they do have a lot of differences, and this chapter is going to uncover them.

Electric vs. stove-top pressure cookers

A major advantage of electric pressure cookers over stove-top appliances is that they are perfect for users who don't have too much time on their hands. Seniors, students, busy parents, regardless of your age or occupation, these appliances are proper time-savers.

Comparison

- While stove-top units have two or more pressure settings, electric cookers feature a more varied maximum pressure

- When using a stove-top pressure cooker, you are the one who adjusts the heat. On the other hand, electric units do it automatically

- A vast majority of stove-top appliances don't have an integrated timer while all electric pressure cookers do

- Even though electric cookers do have a longer release time than stove-top appliances, the thermos-like construction improves the efficiency of the unit by keeping the heat from the coil inside the cooker instead of dissipating it all over your kitchen

Advantages of electric pressure cookers

Although it is easy to assume electric and stove-top cookers are almost the same, they have multiple differences (as shown above).

If you're wondering whether you made the right choice by opting for Instant pot or some similar pressure cooker, the benefits listed below will prove you made a great decision.

Benefits of electric pressure cookers include:

- 5-in-1 kitchen unit
- eight one-key operation buttons for the most frequent cooking tasks
- Convenience
- Delayed cooking option to allow you to plan the meal ahead of time
- Designed to avoid or eliminate potential safety problems
- Fully insulated housing
- Integrated heat source
- Programmable electric control capability

Instant pot and similar appliances pose as the future of healthy and convenient cooking. When it comes to convenience, Instant pot is an absolute winner.

As a vegetarian, you are looking for different ways to make your meals while retaining the benefits of the ingredients, and the Instant pot is an ideal solution for your needs.

Health Benefits Of Pressure Cooking

Electric pressure cookers fit perfectly into a healthy lifestyle. After all, homemade meals prepared in a healthy way are way better than processed items that a lot of people consume nowadays. Throughout this chapter, you'll learn more about the health benefits you can expect by preparing your food in a pressure cooker.

Digestibility

Pressure cookers make absorption easy for your body. How? The combination of pressure and steam can make even the hardest or toughest ingredients tender and succulent. Tenderness is the best indicator that food is easy to digest.

Consistent results

During pressure cooking, heat is evenly, quickly, and deeply distributed regardless of the volume of water or the amount of food in the pot. Naturally, this is important for the digestibility of food.

Stress relief

Simple actions such are preparing ingredients and making all sorts of meals can be relaxing and allow you to manage stress more effectively. During this time, you focus on ingredients, water level, temperature, pressure, and other parts of pressure cooking.

As a result, your mind isn't stuck with issues and problems that you're facing. It is a well-known fact that the more you think about some stressful situation, the worse it seems. Pressure cooking is a great way to eliminate stress after a long, exhausting day at work. This is particularly important if you bear in mind that unresolved stress is bad news for your health.

Dessert won't sabotage your healthy lifestyle.

A vegetarian diet doesn't mean you should avoid desserts, but the problem is that most desserts are unhealthy. With a pressure cooker, you can treat yourself with cakes and other delicious desserts without sabotaging your healthy lifestyle. This way, you won't gain weight or deal with other consequences that come with unhealthy treats at the end of the day.

Heart health

Instant Pot or some other electric pressure cooker supports heart health due to the fact it retains the nutritional value of ingredients you use. Also, the food is prepared in a healthy manner, without frying or other methods that cause weight gain and increase the risk of cardiovascular diseases.

Arthritis relief

Plant-based diet exhibits anti-inflammatory effects, and it helps alleviate pain while supplying the body with much-needed nutrients. Again, this is where pressure cooker steps in; it retains the nutritional value of ingredients and enables you to obtain more vitamins, fiber, minerals, enzymes, and other compounds than you would in any other way.

In addition, electric pressure cookers are fast. You don't have to spend too much time in the kitchen, which alleviates pressure on your joints.

Now that you know more about the important health benefits of pressure cooking and the significance of a vegetarian diet, you're ready to start cooking. Get your Instant Pot ready and choose what meal you're going to make from the vast selection of recipes from this book.

Vitamins and minerals are NOT destroyed

Pressure cookers, regardless of the type, destroy vitamins and minerals. That's a common belief, but the reality is entirely different.

You will be surprised to know that more vitamins and minerals are retained through pressure cooking than with other cooking methods such as steaming or boiling.

The process saves and reuses the cooking liquid, thus providing the maximum vitamin/mineral retention.

No carcinogens

Some cooking methods, such as grilling or frying, produce carcinogens that could jeopardize your health. Pressure cooking is different!

Unlike other high-heat cooking methods, pressure cooking doesn't produce carcinogenic compounds like acrylamide.

It is important to mention that starchy foods are usually the ones that develop carcinogenic compounds when handled at temperatures above 248°F.

Even though Instant pot and similar appliances can go even higher than this temperature, they still don't produce carcinogens due to the moist environment.

A group of researchers discovered that compared to other high-temperature cooking methods, 20 minutes of pressure cooking did not induce the formation of acrylamides in potatoes.

POULTRY RECIPES

1 - Family Dinner Chicken

Serves: 6   Cooking Time: 25 minutes   Preparation Time: 15 minutes

Ingredients:

- 2 tbsp. olive oil
- 1 tsp. garlic powder
- 1 tsp. paprika
- Salt and freshly ground black pepper, to taste
- 1 (2½-lb.) whole chicken, neck and giblets removed
- 1 lemon, cut into 4 wedges
- 1 C. chicken broth

Instructions:

1) In a small bowl, mix together the oil, spices, salt and black pepper.
2) Insert lemon wedges inside the cavity of chicken.
3) Coat the top part of chicken with oil mixture generously.
4) Select "Sauté" of Instant Pot. Then place the chicken, breast side down and cook for about 3-4 minutes.
5) Now, coat the bottom side of the chicken with remaining spice mixture.
6) Flip the chicken and cook for about 1 minute more.
7) Select "Cancel" and transfer the chicken onto a plate.
8) Now, arrange the trivet in the bottom of Instant Pot and pour the broth.
9) Place the chicken on top of trivet, breast side down.
10) Secure the lid and place the pressure valve to "Seal" position.
11) Select "Manual" and cook under "High Pressure" for about 20 minutes.
12) Select "Cancel" and do a "Natural" release.
13) Remove the lid and place chicken onto a cutting board for about 10 minutes before carving.
14) With a sharp knife, cut chicken into desires sized pieces and serve.

Nutrition Information:
Calories per serving: 409; Carbohydrates: 0.9g; Protein: 55.7g; Fat: 19g; Sugar: 0.3g; Sodium: 317mg; Fiber: 0.3g

2 – Popular Chicken Cacciatore

Serves: 4   Cooking Time: 30 minutes   Preparation Time: 15 minutes

Ingredients:

- 2 tbsp. extra-virgin olive oil
- 4 (6-oz.) bone-in, skin-on chicken thighs
- 1 (4-oz.) package sliced fresh mushrooms
- 3 celery stalks, chopped
- ½ of onion, chopped
- 2 garlic cloves, minced
- 1 (14-oz.) can stewed tomatoes
- 2 tbsp. tomato paste
- 2 tsp. Herbes de Provence
- 3 chicken bouillon cubes, crumbled
- ¾ C. water
- Pinch of red pepper flakes
- Freshly ground black pepper, to taste

Instructions:

1) Place the oil in Instant Pot and select "Sauté". Then add the chicken thighs and cook for about 5-6 minutes per side.
2) With a slotted spoon, transfer chicken thighs onto a plate.
3) In the pot, add the mushrooms, celery and onion and cook for about 5 minutes.
4) Add the garlic and cook for about 2 minutes.
5) Select "Cancel" and stir in the chicken, tomatoes, tomato paste, Herbes de Provence, bouillon cubes and water.
6) Secure the lid and place the pressure valve to "Seal" position.
7) Select "Manual" and cook under "High Pressure" for about 11 minutes.
8) Select "Cancel" and carefully do a "Quick" release.
9) Remove the lid and stir in red pepper flakes and black pepper.

Nutrition Information:

Calories per serving: 430; Carbohydrates: 9.2g; Protein: 52.1g; Fat: 20.2g; Sugar: 5.3g; Sodium: 631mg; Fiber: 2.4g

3 – Famous Chicken Piccata

Serves: 4   Cooking Time: 16 minutes   Preparation Time: 15 minutes

Ingredients:

- 4 (6-oz.) skinless, boneless chicken breasts
- Salt and freshly ground black pepper, to taste
- 1 tbsp. extra-virgin olive oil
- 1 C. low-sodium chicken broth
- ¼ C. fresh lemon juice
- 2 tbsp. cold butter
- 2 tbsp. brined capers, drained
- 2 tbsp. fresh parsley, chopped

Instructions:

1) Season the chicken breasts with salt and black pepper evenly.
2) Place the oil in Instant Pot and select "Sauté". Then add the chicken and cook for about 2-3 minutes per side.
3) Select "Cancel" and pour in the broth.
4) Secure the lid and place the pressure valve to "Seal" position.
5) Select "Manual" and cook under "High Pressure" for about 3 minutes.
6) Select "Cancel" and carefully do a "Quick" release.
7) Remove the lid and with tongs, transfer the chicken breasts onto a serving platter.
8) With a piece of foil, cover the chicken breasts to keep warm.
9) Select "Sauté" of Instant Pot and stir in the lemon juice.
10) Cook for about 5-7 minutes.
11) Select "Cancel" and add in the butter, beating continuously.
12) Stir in the capers and parsley and pour the sauce over chicken.
13) Serve immediately.

Nutrition Information:

Calories per serving: 303; Carbohydrates: 0.9g; Protein: 38.8g; Fat: 15.5g; Sugar: 0.4g; Sodium: 289mg; Fiber: 0.3g

4 - Flavorsome Caprese Chicken

Serves: 6   Cooking Time: 15 minutes   Preparation Time: 15 minutes

Ingredients:
- ¼ C. chicken broth
- ¼ C. balsamic vinegar
- ¼ C. maple syrup
- 6 (4-oz.) boneless, skinless chicken breasts
- 8 mozzarella cheese slices
- 3 C. cherry tomatoes, halved
- ½ C. fresh basil leaves, torn

Instructions:

1) In the pot of Instant Pot, place the broth, vinegar and maple syrup and stir to combine.
2) Add the chicken breasts and stir to combine.
3) Secure the lid and place the pressure valve to "Seal" position.
4) Select "Manual" and cook under "High Pressure" for about 8 minutes.
5) Meanwhile, preheat the oven to broiler.
6) Select "Cancel" and carefully do a "Quick" release.
7) Remove the lid of Instant pot and with a slotted spoon, transfer the chicken breasts onto a baking sheet.
8) Place a slice of cheese on each chicken breast.
9) Select "Sauté" of Instant Pot and cook for about 4-5 minutes.
10) Stir in the tomatoes and cook for about 1-2 minutes.
11) Stir in the basil and select "Cancel".
12) Meanwhile, broil the chicken breasts for about 2-3 minutes or until cheese is melted.
13) Divide the chicken breasts onto serving plates and serve with the topping of tomato sauce.

Nutrition Information:
Calories per serving: 377; Carbohydrates: 13.8g; Protein: 54.7g; Fat: 15.4g; Sugar: 10.3g; Sodium: 362mg; Fiber: 1.1g

5 - Purely Greek Flavored Chicken

Serves: 8   Cooking Time: 18 minutes   Preparation Time: 15 minutes

Ingredients:

- 1 tbsp. garlic and herb seasoning
- ½ tsp. garlic salt
- ¼ tsp. ground black pepper
- 2 lb. skinless, boneless chicken breasts
- 2 tbsp. avocado oil
- 6 roasted garlic cloves, mashed
- 1 (8 oz.) jar marinated artichoke hearts, drained
- 1 C. sliced Kalamata olives
- ½ of medium red onion, sliced
- ½ of (16 fluid oz.) bottle Greek salad dressing
- 1 tbsp. arrowroot starch
- 1 (4-oz.) package feta cheese, crumbled

Instructions:

1) In a bowl, mix together the garlic and herb seasoning, garlic salt, and black pepper.Season each chicken breast with seasoning mixture evenly.
2) Place the oil in Instant Pot and select "Sauté". Then add the garlic and cook for about 1 minute.
3) Place the chicken breasts and cook for about 2 minutes per side.
4) Select "Cancel" and place the artichoke hearts and olives around and top of the chicken breasts.
5) Top with onion, followed by dressing.
6) Secure the lid and place the pressure valve to "Seal" position.
7) Select "Manual" and cook under "High Pressure" for about 15 minutes.
8) Select "Cancel" and carefully do a "Quick" release.
9) Remove the lid of Instant pot and with a slotted spoon, transfer the chicken breasts onto a plate.
10) In the pot, add the arrowroot starch and beat until well combined.
11) Stir in the cooked chicken and select "Sauté".
12) Cook for about 3 minutes.
13) Select "Cancel" and serve hot with the topping of feta cheese.

Nutrition Information:

Calories per serving: 406; Carbohydrates: 8.2g; Protein: 28.7g; Fat: 29.3g; Sugar: 1.2g; Sodium: 572mg; Fiber: 2.5g

6 – Braised Chicken

Serves: 4   Cooking Time: 18 minutes   Preparation Time: 15 minutes

Ingredients:

- 8 (4-oz.) skinless, boneless chicken thighs
- Salt, to taste
- 2 tbsp. olive oil
- 2 oz. pancetta, chopped
- ½ of large red onion, sliced
- 2 garlic cloves, chopped
- ½ C. dry white wine
- 1 C. red peppers, seeded and sliced
- 1 C. sliced pickled roasted peppers
- 2 fresh rosemary sprigs
- 2 tbsp. balsamic vinegar
- 2 tbsp. fresh lemon juice
- 1 oz. butter

Instructions:

1) Season the chicken thighs with salt evenly and set aside.
2) Place the oil in Instant Pot and select "Sauté". Then add 4 chicken thighs and cook for about 1-2 minutes per side.
3) With a slotted spoon, transfer the chicken thighs onto a plate.
4) Repeat with the remaining chicken thighs.
5) In the pot, add the pancetta, onion and garlic and cook for about 1-2 minutes. Add the wine and cook for about 1 minute, scraping up the browned bits from the bottom.
6) Select "Cancel" and stir in the remaining ingredients except for butter.
7) Place the cooked chicken thighs on top and gently, cover with some of onions and peppers. Secure the lid and place the pressure valve to "Seal" position. Select "Manual" and cook under "High Pressure" for about 10 minutes. Select "Cancel" and carefully do a "Quick" release.
8) Remove the lid and with a slotted spoon, transfer the chicken thighs onto a plate. Select "Sauté" and cook for about 5 minutes.
9) Add the butter and stir until melted completely.
10) Select "Cancel" and pour the sauce over chicken thighs. Serve immediately.

Nutrition Information:

Calories per serving: 539; Carbohydrates: 10.1g; Protein: 57.7g; Fat: 27.2g; Sugar: 5.2g; Sodium: 499mg; Fiber: 1.6g

7 – Moroccan Chicken Meal

Serves: 6   Cooking Time: 20 minutes   Preparation Time: 15 minutes

Ingredients:

- 1 tbsp. oil
- 2 lb. boneless chicken thighs, trimmed and cut into large chunks
- 2 red peppers, cut into chunks
- 1 large onion
- 4 garlic cloves
- 2 Roma tomatoes, cut into chunks
- 1 (15-oz.) can chickpeas, rinsed and drained
- 1 tsp. salt
- ½ tsp. freshly ground black pepper
- 1 tsp. ground cumin
- ½ tsp. ground coriander
- 1 tsp. dried parsley
- ½ tsp. za'atar
- 1 C. tomato sauce

Instructions:

1) Place the oil in Instant Pot and select "Sauté". Then add the onion and garlic and cook for about 5 minutes.
2) Add the chicken chunks, and cook for about 3-5 minutes or browned from all sides.
3) Select "Cancel" and stir in the remaining ingredients.
4) Secure the lid and place the pressure valve to "Seal" position.
5) Select "Manual" and cook under "High Pressure" for about 10 minutes.
6) Select "Cancel" and carefully do a "Quick" release.
7) Remove the lid and serve hot.

Nutrition Information:
Calories per serving: 430; Carbohydrates: 24.4g; Protein: 48.9g; Fat: 14.6g; Sugar: 4.7g; Sodium: 949mg; Fiber: 5.1g

8 – Saucy Chicken

Serves: 6   Cooking Time: 25 minutes   Preparation Time: 15 minutes

Ingredients:

- 2 tbsp. extra-virgin olive oil
- 2 lb. chicken breast, cut into bite-sized pieces
- 1 lemon, peeled and sliced very thinly
- 2 C. green olives, pitted
- 2 red peppers, seeded and cut into long, wide, strips
- 2 orange peppers, seeded and cut into long, wide strips
- 2 onions, quartered
- 8 garlic cloves, chopped
- 2 tbsp. tomato paste
- 2 tbsp. Dijon Mustard
- 1 tbsp. molasses
- 1 tbsp. honey
- 1 tsp. ground cumin
- 1 tsp. ground turmeric
- ½ tsp. ground ginger
- ½ tsp. ground cinnamon
- ½ tsp. salt
- ½ tsp. freshly ground black pepper

Instructions:

1) Place the oil in Instant Pot and select "Sauté". Then add the chicken pieces and cook for about 3-5 minutes or browned from all sides.
2) Select "Cancel" and stir in the remaining ingredients.
3) Secure the lid and place the pressure valve to "Seal" position.
4) Select "Manual" and cook under "High Pressure" for about 20 minutes.
5) Select "Cancel" and carefully do a "Quick" release.
6) Remove the lid and serve hot.

Nutrition Information:

Calories per serving: 343; Carbohydrates: 21.2g; Protein: 34.5g; Fat: 13.9g; Sugar: 11.1g; Sodium: 732mg; Fiber: 4.1g

9 – Healthier Chicken Dinner

Serves: 4   Cooking Time: 20 minutes   Preparation Time: 15 minutes

Ingredients:

- 1 bunch mustard greens, washed and chopped
- 4 boneless, skinless chicken thighs
- Salt and freshly ground black pepper, to taste
- 3 garlic cloves, minced
- ½ C. green olives, pitted
- ½ C. cherry tomatoes
- 1 tsp. Dijon mustard
- 1 tsp. honey
- 1 C. white wine
- 1/3 C. extra-virgin olive oil
- 2 tbsp. fresh lemon juice

Instructions:

1) In the pot of Instant pot, place greens and top with chicken thighs.
2) Sprinkle with salt and black pepper.
3) Top with garlic, followed by olives, tomatoes, mustard and honey.
4) Place the wine, oil and lemon juice on top evenly.
5) Secure the lid and place the pressure valve to "Seal" position.
6) Select "Manual" and cook under "High Pressure" for about 15 minutes.
7) Select "Cancel" and carefully do a "Quick" release.
8) Remove the lid and serve hot.

Nutrition Information:

Calories per serving: 526; Carbohydrates: 11.5g; Protein: 44.7g; Fat: 29.5g; Sugar: 4.5g; Sodium: 356mg; Fiber:4.70g

10 - Inspiring Chicken Drumsticks

Serves: 4   Cooking Time: 20 minutes   Preparation Time: 15 minutes

Ingredients:

- 1 tbsp. olive oil
- 1½ red onions, peeled, halved and cut into wedges
- 1½ tsp. salt
- 8 skin-on chicken drumsticks
- ½ tsp. freshly ground black pepper
- ¼ tsp. red chili powder
- 8 garlic cloves, peeled
- 2 tbsp. dried thyme leaves
- ½ tsp. lemon zest, grated
- 2/3 C. canned diced tomatoes
- 2 tbsp. sweet balsamic vinegar

Instructions:

1) Place the oil in Instant Pot and select "Sauté". Then add the onions and ½ tsp. of salt and cook for about 3 minutes.
2) Add the chicken drumsticks with salt, black pepper and red chili powder and cook for about 1 minute per side.
3) Select "Cancel" and place the garlic cloves on top of chicken drumsticks, followed by thyme, lemon zest and tomatoes evenly.
4) Drizzle with vinegar evenly.
5) Secure the lid and place the pressure valve to "Seal" position.
6) Select "Poultry" and just use the default time of 15 minutes.
7) Select "Cancel" and do a "Natural" release for about 3 minutes, then do a "Quick" release.
8) Remove the lid and stir the mixture.
9) Serve hot.

Nutrition Information:

Calories per serving: 547; Carbohydrates: 8.2g; Protein: 79.2g; Fat: 20g; Sugar: 2.7g; Sodium: 1100mg; Fiber: 2g

11 - Balanced Spicy Chicken

Serves: 8   Cooking Time: 21 minutes   Preparation Time: 15 minutes

Ingredients:

For Spice Blend:
- 1 tsp. paprika
- 1 tsp. ground ginger
- 1 tsp. ground cumin
- 1 tsp. ground coriander
- ½ tsp. ground turmeric
- ½ tsp. ground cinnamon
- ½ tsp. ground allspice
- ½ tsp. kosher salt

For Chicken:
- 1 tbsp. olive oil
- 1 red onion, sliced
- 3 garlic cloves, chopped
- 1 C. low-sodium chicken broth
- 1 C. pitted green olives
- ½ C. raisins
- ½ of lemon, seeded and sliced thinly
- 3 lb. boneless, skinless chicken thighs
- ¼ C. fresh parsley, chopped

Instructions:

1) For spice blend: in a small bowl, mix together all ingredients. Set aside.
2) Place the oil in Instant Pot and select "Sauté". Then add the onion and garlic and cook for about 5 minutes.
3) Stir in the spice blend and cook for about 1 minute.
4) Add the broth and scrape up the browned bits from bottom.
5) Select "Cancel" and stir in the olives, raisins, lemon slices, and chicken thighs.
6) Secure the lid and place the pressure valve to "Seal" position.
7) Select "Poultry" and just use the default time of 15 minutes.
8) Select "Cancel" and carefully do a "Quick" release.
9) Remove the lid and serve hot.

Nutrition Information:
Calories per serving: 398; Carbohydrates: 10.8g; Protein: 50.3g; Fat: 16.3g; Sugar: 6g; Sodium: 452mg; Fiber: 1.5g

12 - Drunken Chicken & Mushrooms

Serves: 6   Cooking Time: 27 minutes   Preparation Time: 15 minutes

Ingredients:

- 3 lb. bone-in chicken thighs
- Salt and freshly ground black pepper, to taste
- ½ C. all-purpose flour
- 3 tbsp. olive oil, divided
- 8 oz. fresh Cremini mushrooms, sliced thickly
- 3 scallions, chopped
- 2 garlic cloves, minced
- ½ C. low-sodium chicken broth
- 1/3 C. sweet Marsala wine
- 1/3 C. heavy whipping cream

Instructions:

1) Season the chicken thighs with salt and black pepper and then coat with flour evenly.
2) Place 2 tbsp. of the oil in Instant Pot and select "Sauté". Then add the chicken thighs and cook for about 2-3 minutes per side. With a slotted spoon, transfer the chicken thighs onto a plate.
3) In the pot, add the remaining oil and cook the mushrooms, scallions and garlic for about 2-3 minutes.
4) Select "Cancel" and stir in the broth.Place the chicken thighs on top.
5) Secure the lid and place the pressure valve to "Seal" position.Select "Manual" and cook under "High Pressure" for about 10 minutes.
6) Select "Cancel" and do a "Natural" release.
7) Remove the lid and with a slotted spoon, transfer the chicken thighs onto a plate.
8) With a piece of foil, cover the chicken thighs to keep warm.Select "Sauté" and stir in the marsala wine.
9) Bring the mushroom mixture to a boil and cook for about 3 minutes.Stir in the heavy whipping cream and cook for about 5 minutes, stirring frequently.
10) Select "Cancel" and pour the mushroom sauce over chicken.
11) Serve immediately.

Nutrition Information:
Calories per serving: 578; Carbohydrates: 11g; Protein: 68.2g; Fat: 26.4g; Sugar: 1g; Sodium: 235mg; Fiber: 0.7g

13 - Creamy Chicken Breasts

Serves: 4   Cooking Time: 13 minutes   Preparation Time: 15 minutes

Ingredients:

- 4 boneless, skinless chicken breasts
- 1 C. low sodium chicken broth
- 1 tsp. garlic, minced
- 1 tsp. Italian seasoning
- Salt and freshly ground black pepper, to taste

- 1/3 C. chopped roasted red peppers
- 1/3 C. heavy cream
- 1½ tbsp. cornstarch
- 1 tbsp. basil pesto

Instructions:

1) In the pot of Instant Pot, place the chicken breasts and top with broth.
2) Sprinkle with garlic, Italian seasoning, salt and black pepper.
3) Secure the lid and place the pressure valve to "Seal" position.
4) Select "Manual" and cook under "High Pressure" for about 8 minutes.
5) Select "Cancel" and do a "Natural" release for about 5 minutes, then do a "Quick" release.
6) Remove the lid and with a slotted spoon, transfer the chicken breasts onto a plate.
7) With a piece of foil, cover the chicken thighs to keep warm.
8) In the pot, add the remaining ingredients and stir until well combined.
9) Select "Sauté" and cook for about 3-4 minutes.
10) Stir in the cooked chicken breasts and select "Cancel".
11) Serve hot.

Nutrition Information:
Calories per serving: 412; Carbohydrates: 11.9g; Protein: 50.2g; Fat: 16.7g; Sugar: 0.8g; Sodium: 244mg; Fiber: 0.3g

14 – 2-Cheeses Chicken

Serves: 4   Cooking Time: 10 minutes   Preparation Time: 15 minutes

Ingredients:

- 4 (6 oz.) boneless, skinless chicken breast halves
- 1 (14½-oz.) can diced tomatoes with juices
- 1 (12-oz.) jar marinated quartered artichoke hearts, undrained
- 2 tsp. Italian seasoning
- ¾ tsp. garlic salt
- 1 C. mozzarella cheese, shredded
- ¼ C. Parmesan cheese, grated

Instructions:

1) In the pot of Instant Pot, place the chicken breast halves and top with tomatoes, followed by the artichokes.
2) Sprinkle with Italian seasoning and garlic salt.
3) Secure the lid and place the pressure valve to "Seal" position.
4) Select "Manual" and cook under "High Pressure" for about 10 minutes.
5) Select "Cancel" and do a "Natural" release for about 10 minutes, then do a "Quick" release.
6) Remove the lid and immediately, sprinkle the chicken mixture with both cheeses.
7) Immediately, cover the instant pot with a lid for about 5 minutes before serving.

Nutrition Information:

Calories per serving: 429; Carbohydrates: 13.8g; Protein: 57g; Fat: 16.1g; Sugar: 3.9g; Sodium: 318mg; Fiber: 5.9g

15 – Low-Carb Dinner Meal

Serves: 8   Cooking Time: 10 minutes   Preparation Time: 15 minutes

Ingredients:

- 4 (8-oz.) boneless, skinless chicken breasts, halved and pounded thinly
- 4 garlic cloves, minced
- 1 tbsp. Italian seasoning blend
- Salt, to taste
- 2 tbsp. extra-virgin olive oil
- 2 tbsp. butter
- ¾ C. heavy whipping cream
- ¼ C. low-sodium chicken broth
- 1 tsp. seasoned salt
- ¾ C. Parmigiano-Reggiano cheese
- ½ C. sun-dried tomatoes
- 2 C. fresh spinach

Instructions:

1) In a large bowl, add the chicken breasts, garlic, Italian seasoning and salt and mix well.
2) Place the oil and butter in Instant Pot and select "Sauté". Then add the chicken breasts and cook for about 1 minute per side.
3) Select "Cancel" and stir in the cream, broth and seasoned salt
4) Secure the lid and place the pressure valve to "Seal" position.
5) Select "Manual" and cook under "High Pressure" for about 1 minute.
6) Select "Cancel" and do a "Natural" release for about 4 minutes, then do a "Quick" release.
7) Remove the lid and stir the mixture well.
8) Select "Sauté" and bring to a gentle simmer.
9) Stir in the cheese and sun-dried tomatoes and cook for about 2-3 minutes.
10) Stir in the spinach and cook for about 1 minute.
11) Select "Cancel" and serve hot.

Nutrition Information:

Calories per serving: 346; Carbohydrates: 1.6g; Protein: 36.5g; Fat: 21.3g; Sugar: 0.4g; Sodium: 386mg; Fiber: 0.3g

16 – Souvlaki Inspired Chicken Bowl

Serves: 4   Cooking Time: 3 minutes   Preparation Time: 20 minutes

Ingredients:

- ½ C. plus 2 tbsp. water, divided
- ¼ C. plus 2 tbsp. olive oil, divided
- 3 garlic cloves, grated and divided
- ½ tsp. dried oregano
- ½ tsp. paprika
- Pinch of crushed red pepper flakes
- Salt and freshly ground black pepper, to taste
- 1½ lb. boneless, skinless chicken breasts, cut into ½-inch thick slices
- 1 C. couscous
- 1 C. full-fat Greek yogurt
- 2 tbsp. fresh lemon juice
- 1 English cucumber, chopped
- 1 C. cherry tomatoes, quartered
- ½ C. Kalamata olives, pitted and chopped
- ½ C. feta cheese, crumbled
- 2 tbsp. fresh dill, chopped

Instructions:

1) In the pot of Instant Pot, ½ C. of the water, ¼ C. of olive oil, 2 garlic cloves, oregano, paprika, red pepper flakes, salt and black pepper and mix well.Add the chicken, slices and stir to combine.Secure the lid and place the pressure valve to "Seal" position.Select "Manual" and cook under "High Pressure" for about 3 minutes.
2) Select "Cancel" and carefully do a "Quick" release.Remove the lid and with a slotted spoon, transfer the chicken slices into a bowl.
3) In the pot, add the couscous, salt and black pepper and stir to combine.
4) With a glass lid, cover the Instant Pot for about 6-7 minutes or until couscous is tender and fluffy.Uncover the pot and with a fork, fluff the couscous.
5) Meanwhile, in a bowl, add the yogurt, lemon juice, remaining garlic and 2 tbsp. water and beat until well combined.In the bottom of each serving plate, divide the yogurt sauce evenly and top with couscous, chicken slices, cucumbers, tomatoes, Kalamata olives, feta and dill.
6) Drizzle with the remaining olive oil and serve.

Nutrition Information:

Calories per serving: 808; Carbohydrates: 46.2g; Protein: 62.5g; Fat: 40.8g; Sugar: 7.8g; Sodium: 123mg; Fiber: 4.1g

17 – Protein-Packed Bowl

Serves: 6   Cooking Time: 6 minutes   Preparation Time: 20 minutes

Ingredients:

For Tzatziki Sauce:
- 1 C. plain Greek yogurt
- 1 cucumber, peeled, seeded and grated
- 1 tbsp. fresh dill weed
- ¾ tsp. seasoned salt
- ¼ tsp. freshly ground black pepper

For Chicken Bowl:
- 1½ C. chicken broth
- 1 C. uncooked quinoa
- 1 lb. boneless chicken breasts, cut into 7-8 pieces
- 2 tsp. Greek seasoning
- Salt and freshly ground black pepper, to taste
- 1 cucumber, quartered
- 1 C. grape tomatoes, halved
- 1 C. Kalamata olives
- 1 (15-oz.) can chickpeas, rinsed and drained

Instructions:

1) For tzatziki sauce: in a bowl, add all ingredients and mix until well combined.Refrigerate until using.
2) In the pot of Instant Pot, place the broth and quinoa and stir to combine.
3) Arrange the chicken breasts on top and sprinkle with the Greek seasoning, salt and black pepper.
4) Secure the lid and place the pressure valve to "Seal" position.
5) Select "Manual" and cook under "High Pressure" for about 6 minutes.
6) Select "Cancel" and carefully do a "Quick" release.
7) Remove the lid and transfer the chicken and quinoa into serving bowls evenly.
8) Top with chickpeas, vegetables and tzatziki sauce evenly.
9) Serve hot.

Nutrition Information:
Calories per serving: 421; Carbohydrates: 44.4g; Protein: 34.2g; Fat: 11.6g; Sugar: 5.5g; Sodium: 340mg; Fiber: 6.8g

18 - Colorful Chicken & Rice Platter

Serves: 6   Cooking Time: 18 minutes   Preparation Time: 15 minutes

Ingredients:

- 2 tbsp. olive oil
- 1½ lb. bone-in, skin-on chicken thighs
- Salt, to taste
- 1 red bell pepper, seeded and chopped
- ½ of onion, sliced
- 3 cloves garlic, minced
- 1 tsp. ground cumin
- 1 tsp. red chili pepper
- 1 tsp. dried oregano
- ½ tsp. ground white pepper
- Pinch of red pepper flakes
- 1 lb. tomatoes, chopped
- 1½ C. chicken broth
- 1 C. long-grain rice
- 1 C. frozen peas, partially thawed

Instructions:

1) Place the oil in Instant Pot and select "Sauté". Then add the chicken thighs and cook for about 3 minutes per side.
2) With a slotted spoon, transfer the chicken thighs onto a plate.
3) In the pot, add the bell pepper, onion, and garlic and cook for about 4-5 minutes.
4) Stir in the tomatoes and chicken broth and bring to a boil.
5) Select "Cancel" and stir in the rice and top with the cooked chicken thighs.
6) Secure the lid and place the pressure valve to "Seal" position.
7) Select "Manual" and cook under "High Pressure" for about 12 minutes.
8) Select "Cancel" and do a "Natural" release.
9) Remove the lid and stir in the peas.
10) Immediately, secure the lid for about 5 minutes before serving.

Nutrition Information:

Calories per serving: 427; Carbohydrates: 3g; Protein: 38.8g; Fat: 14g; Sugar: 4.9g; Sodium: 342mg; Fiber: 3.5g

19 – Tuscan Chicken Rice

Serves: 3   Cooking Time: 15 minutes   Preparation Time: 15 minutes

Ingredients:

- 1 C. rice
- 1½ C. chicken broth
- 3 boneless, skinless chicken breast
- 1/3 C. basil pesto
- ½ C. chopped marinated artichoke hearts in oil strain the oil
- ½ C. sun-dried tomatoes in oil
- 1 C. mozzarella cheese
- 1 tbsp. Italian seasoning

Instructions:

1) In the pot of Instant Pot, place the rice and chicken broth.
2) Arrange the chicken breasts over rice in a single layer
3) Spread the pesto over each chicken breast evenly.
4) Top with the artichoke hearts, followed by ¼ C. of the sun-dried tomatoes, cheese, and remaining sun-dried tomatoes.
5) Sprinkle with the Italian seasoning.
6) Secure the lid and place the pressure valve to "Seal" position.
7) Select "Manual" and cook under "High Pressure" for about 15 minutes.
8) Select "Cancel" and do a "Natural" release.
9) Remove the lid and stir the mixture.
10) Serve hot.

Nutrition Information:

Calories per serving: 471; Carbohydrates: 55.8g; Protein: 41.1g; Fat: 7.8g; Sugar: 2g; Sodium: 553mg; Fiber: 3.2g

20 – Favorite Italian Chicken Pasta

Serves: 6   Cooking Time: 10 minutes   Preparation Time: 15 minutes

Ingredients:

- 1 tbsp. olive oil
- ½ C. onion, chopped
- 1 tbsp. garlic, minced
- 1¾ C. chicken broth
- 8 oz. uncooked penne pasta
- 1½ lb. chicken tenderloins, cut into slices
- 1 tsp. Italian seasoning
- Salt and freshly ground black pepper, to taste
- 1 (24-oz.) jar tomato-based pasta sauce
- 1 (8-oz.) package cream cheese
- 3 C. fresh spinach, chopped
- 2-3 tbsp. cornstarch
- 3 tbsp. water
- 6 tbsp. Parmesan cheese, shredded

Instructions:

1) Place the oil in Instant Pot and select "Sauté". Then add the onion and cook for about 3-4 minutes.
2) Add the garlic and cook for about 1 minute.
3) Select "Cancel" and stir in the broth.
4) Place the pasta in a single layer, followed by the chicken slices.
5) Sprinkle with Italian seasoning, salt and black pepper.
6) Top with pasta sauce evenly, followed by the cream cheese block.
7) Secure the lid and place the pressure valve to "Seal" position.
8) Select "Manual" and cook under "High Pressure" for about 4 minutes.
9) Select "Cancel" and do a "Natural" release for about 5 minutes, then do a "Quick" release.
10) Meanwhile, in a bowl, dissolve cornstarch in water.
11) Remove the lid and stir in the spinach.
12) In the pot, add the cornstarch, beating continuously.
13) Select "sauté" and cook for about 1 minute, stirring continuously.
14) Select "Cancel" and serve hot with the topping of cheese.

Nutrition Information:

Calories per serving: 629; Carbohydrates: 42.2g; Protein: 45.9g; Fat: 29.9g; Sugar: 10.9g; Sodium: 1023mg; Fiber: 3.5g

RED MEAT RECIPES

21 – Flavorful Chuck Shoulder

Serves: 6   Cooking Time: 45 minutes   Preparation Time: 15 minutes

Ingredients:

- 2 lb. boneless beef chuck roast, trimmed and cut into 2" size cubes against the grain
- 3 tbsp. all-purpose flour
- ½ tsp. dried oregano
- Salt and freshly ground black pepper, to taste
- 1 large onion, chopped finely
- 4 shallots, sliced
- 2 tbsp. extra-virgin olive oil
- 1 garlic clove, minced
- ½ C. Medjool dates, pitted and chopped
- ½ C. beef broth
- ¼ C. balsamic vinegar
- ¼ C. red wine

Instructions:

1) In a bowl, mix together the flour, oregano, salt and black pepper.
2) In a sealable plastic bag, add the beef cubes and flour mixture.
3) Seal the bag and shake to coat evenly.
4) Place the oil in Instant Pot and select "Sauté". Then add the beef mixture, onions, shallots and garlic and cook for about 4-5 minutes.
5) Select "Cancel" and stir in the remaining ingredients.
6) Secure the lid and place the pressure valve to "Seal" position.
7) Select "Manual" and cook under "High Pressure" for about 40 minutes.
8) Select "Cancel" and do a "Natural" release.
9) Remove the lid and serve hot.

Nutrition Information:
Calories per serving: 408; Carbohydrates: 18.9g; Protein: 47.5g; Fat: 14.3g; Sugar: 11.2g; Sodium: 194mg; Fiber: 1.7g

22 - Yummy Chuck Roast

Serves: 6   Cooking Time: 1 hour 10 minutes   Preparation Time: 15 minutes

Ingredients:

- 1 tsp. Swerve sweetener
- 2 tsp. red chili powder
- 1 tsp. paprika
- ½ tsp. cayenne powder
- 1 tbsp. ground cumin
- 1 tbsp. onion powder
- 1 tsp. ground cinnamon
- Salt and freshly ground black pepper, to taste
- 3 lb. chuck roast, cut in to large chunks
- 3 garlic cloves, slivered
- 1 tbsp. olive oil
- 1 C. beef broth

Instructions:

1) In a small bowl, mix together the Swerve, spices, salt and black pepper.
2) With a sharp knife, cut little slits into the roast.
3) Stuff the garlic slivers into roast slits evenly.
4) Now, cut the roast into 6 even chunks.
5) Rub each roast chunk with spice mixture evenly.
6) Place the oil in Instant Pot and select "Sauté". Then add the roast chunks and cook for about 8-10 minutes or until browned completely.
7) Select "Cancel" and stir in the broth.
8) Secure the lid and place the pressure valve to "Seal" position.
9) Select "Manual" and cook under "High Pressure" for about 60 minutes.
10) Select "Cancel" and do a "Natural" release.
11) Remove the lid and transfer the roast chunks onto a cutting board.
12) Cut each chunk into small pieces and serve.

Nutrition Information:

Calories per serving: 531; Carbohydrates: 3.9g; Protein: 76.3g; Fat: 21.9g; Sugar: 1.5g; Sodium: 316mg; Fiber: 0.9g

23 – Nourishing Dinner Beef

Serves: 3   Cooking Time: 35 minutes   Preparation Time: 15 minutes

Ingredients:

- 4 dates, pitted and soaked in warm water
- 4 tbsp. sun-dried tomatoes in oil
- 1 lb. beef chuck roast
- 2 tbsp. olive oil
- 1 tbsp. shallot, minced
- 4 garlic cloves, minced
- 1 tsp. dried oregano
- 1 tsp. dried thyme
- Salt and freshly ground black pepper, to taste
- 1 tbsp. balsamic vinegar
- 1 C. chicken broth
- 1 tsp. lemon zest, grated

Instructions:

1) In a food processor, add the dates and sun-dried tomatoes and pulse until smooth. Transfer the date puree into a bowl and set aside.
2) Place the oil in Instant Pot and select "Sauté". Then add the shallot and garlic and cook for about 1 minute.
3) Add the beef and sear for about 2 minutes per side.
4) Select "Cancel" and stir in the remaining ingredients except for lemon zest.
5) Secure the lid and place the pressure valve to "Seal" position.
6) Select "Manual" and cook under "High Pressure" for about 30 minutes.
7) Select "Cancel" and do a "Natural" release.
8) Remove the lid and transfer the meat into a bowl.
9) With 2 forks, shred the beef.
10) Garnish with lemon zest and serve.

Nutrition Information:

Calories per serving: 705; Carbohydrates: 13.4g; Protein: 42.3g; Fat: 53.3g; Sugar: 7.4g; Sodium: 428mg; Fiber: 1.9g

24 – Italian Zesty Beef

Serves: 8   Cooking Time: 1 hour   Preparation Time: 15 minutes

Ingredients:

- 3 lb. beef chuck roast, cut into large chunks
- ½ (16-oz.) jar mild Pepperoncini
- 1 (1-oz.) packet zesty Italian dressing mix
- 1 tsp. dried oregano
- 1 tsp. dried basil
- 4 garlic cloves, minced
- 1/3 C. Pepperoncini Juice from the Jar
- 1 (10½-oz.) can beef broth
- ¼ C. red wine

Instructions:

1) In the pot of Instant Pot, place all the ingredients and stir to combine.
2) Secure the lid and place the pressure valve to "Seal" position.
3) Select "Manual" and cook under "High Pressure" for about 60 minutes.
4) Select "Cancel" and do a "Natural" release.
5) Remove the lid and transfer the meat into a bowl.
6) With 2 forks, shred the beef and serve.

Nutrition Information:

Calories per serving: 648; Carbohydrates: 4.2g; Protein: 45.5g; Fat: 47.7g; Sugar: 0.2g; Sodium: 599mg; Fiber: 0.1g

25 – Family Friendly Meatballs Spaghetti

Serves: 5   Cooking Time: 11 minutes   Preparation Time: 20 minutes

Ingredients:

- 2/3 C. water
- 1/3 C. uncooked quinoa
- 1 lb. Italian sausage
- 2 garlic cloves, finely minced
- 1½ tsp. dried oregano
- 1 tsp. dried basil
- ½ tsp. dried parsley
- 1½ tsp. granulated onion powder
- ½ tsp. salt
- 1 (24-oz.) bottle tomato basil marinara sauce
- 1 (12-oz.) package spaghetti
- 2 tbsp. fresh basil, chopped

Instructions:

1) In the pot of Instant Pot, place quinoa and water.Secure the lid and place the pressure valve to "Seal" position.
2) Select "Manual" and cook under "High Pressure" for about 1 minute. Select "Cancel" and do a "Natural" release for about 10 minutes, then do a "Quick" release.
3) Remove the lid and transfer the quinoa into a bowl. Set aside to cool slightly. In the bowl of quinoa, add the sausage, garlic, herbs, oregano, onion powder and salt and with your hands, mix until well combined.
4) Make about 2-inch ball from the mixture.
5) In the bottom of Instant Pot, place half of marinara sauce.
6) Arrange the meatballs over the sauce and top with the remaining sauce.
7) Secure the lid and place the pressure valve to "Seal" position.
8) Select "Manual" and cook under "High Pressure" for about 10 minutes.
9) Meanwhile, in a pan of the lightly salted boiling water, cook the spaghetti for about 8-10 minutes or according to package directions.
10) Drain the spaghetti for and rinse under cold running water.
11) Divide the spaghetti onto serving plates.
12) Select "Cancel" of Instant Pot and carefully do a "Quick" release.
13) Remove the lid and place the meatballs sauce over spaghetti onto each plate.
14) Garnish with basil and serve.

Nutrition Information:
Calories per serving: 669; Carbohydrates: 64.5g; Protein: 29.6g; Fat: 31.7g; Sugar: 12.3g; Sodium: 1480mg; Fiber: 4.6g

26 – Lombard Osso Buco

Serves: 4   Cooking Time: 1 hour 33 minutes   Preparation Time: 15 minutes

Ingredients:

- 4 fresh thyme sprigs
- 2 fresh rosemary sprigs
- 1 bay leaf
- 4 (10-oz.) bone-in veal shanks, patted dry
- Salt and freshly ground black pepper, to taste
- ½ C. all-purpose flour
- 3 tbsp. extra-virgin olive oil
- 2 tbsp. unsalted butter
- 2 medium carrots, peeled and cut into ¼-inch pieces
- 1 onion, cut into ¼-inch pieces
- 1 celery stalk, cut into ¼-inch pieces
- 4 garlic cloves, sliced thinly
- ½ tsp. tomato paste
- ½ C. dry white wine
- ½ C. chicken broth
- 1 (14½-oz.) can diced tomatoes, drained

Instructions:

1) With a kitchen twine tie the herb sprigs and bay leaf. Season the veal shanks with salt and black pepper and then coat with the flour evenly.
2) Place the oil in Instant Pot and select "Sauté". Then add the shanks in 2 batches and cook for about 5-7 minutes per side. With a slotted spoon, transfer the shank onto a plate.
3) In the pot, add the butter, carrot, onion and celery and cook for about 6-8 minutes. Stir in the garlic and tomato paste, and cook for about 1-2 minutes.
4) Add the wine and scrape the browned bits from the bottom. Select "Cancel" and stir in the broth. Submerge the cooked shanks into veggie mixture and place the herb bag on top. Secure the lid and place the pressure valve to "Seal" position.
5) Select "Manual" and cook under "High Pressure" for about 40 minutes.
6) Select "Cancel" and do a "Natural" release. Remove the lid and with a slotted spoon, transfer the shank onto a plate.
7) Select "Sauté" and cook for about 10-15 minutes or until desired thickness of sauce. Select "Cancel" and let the sauce sit for at least 10 minutes. With a slotted spoon, remove any excess fat off the top.
8) Transfer the osso buco onto a serving platter and top with the sauce. Serve immediately.

Nutrition Information:

Calories per serving: 816; Carbohydrates: 23.7g; Protein: 93.4g; Fat: 34.4g; Sugar: 5.9g; Sodium: 472mg; Fiber: 3.2g

27 – Favorite Greek Dinner

Serves: 10   Cooking Time: 1 hour 2 minutes   Preparation Time: 15 minutes

Ingredients:

For Lamb:
- 2 tbsp. extra-virgin olive oil
- 5 lb. boneless leg of lamb
- 3 garlic cloves, minced
- 1 bay leaf, crushed
- 1 tsp. dried marjoram
- 1 tsp. dried thyme
- 1 tsp. dried sage
- 1 tsp. ground ginger
- 1 tsp. sea salt
- ½ tsp. ground black pepper
- 2 C. beef broth
- 2½-3 lb. potatoes, peeled and cut into 2-inch pieces

For Gravy:
- 2/3 tbsp. arrowroot powder
- 1/3 C. water

Instructions:

1) Place the oil in Instant Pot and select "Sauté". Then add the leg of lamb and sear for about 4-5 minutes per side.
2) Select "Cancel" and stir in the garlic, herbs, salt, black pepper and broth. Secure the lid and place the pressure valve to "Seal" position.
3) Select "Manual" and cook under "High Pressure" for about 50 minutes. Select "Cancel" and carefully do a "Quick" release. Remove the lid and stir in the potatoes.
4) Secure the lid and place the pressure valve to "Seal" position. Select "Manual" and cook under "High Pressure" for about 10 minutes.
5) Select "Cancel" and carefully do a "Quick" release. Remove the lid and with a slotted spoon, transfer the potatoes and lamb meat onto a serving platter.
6) With a piece of foil, cover the meat and potatoes to keep them warm. For gravy: in a small bowl, dissolve the arrowroot powder in water.
7) In the pot, add the arrowroot powder mixture, beating continuously.
8) Select "Sauté" and cook for about 1-2 minutes.
9) Cut the meat into desired-sized pieces.
10) Divide meat and potatoes onto serving plates.
11) Pour sauce on top and serve.

Nutrition Information:
Calories per serving: 537; Carbohydrates: 19.2g; Protein: 66.7g; Fat: 19.8g; Sugar:1.5; Sodium: 520mg; Fiber: 2.9g

28 – Aromatic Leg of Lamb

Serves: 8   Cooking Time: 1¾ hours   Preparation Time: 15 minutes

Ingredients:

- 1 (4-4½-lb.) boneless leg of lamb, string mesh removed
- 6-8 garlic cloves, cut into slivers
- 2 tbsp. olive oil
- Salt and freshly cracked black pepper, to taste
- 1 tsp. garlic powder
- 1 tsp. paprika
- 1 onion, peeled and quartered
- 2 garlic cloves, smashed
- 1 C. dry white wine
- 7-10 thyme sprigs
- 3 rosemary sprigs
- 1 oregano sprig
- 2 tsp. dried oregano
- 2 bay leaves
- 1¼ C. chicken broth
- ¼ C. fresh lemon juice

Instructions:

1) With a sharp knife, cut little slits into the leg of lamb. Stuff the garlic slivers into meat slits evenly.
2) Drizzle the lamb with 1 tbsp. of olive oil and season with the garlic powder, paprika, salt and pepper.
3) Place the remaining oil in the Instant Pot and select "Sauté". Then add the lamb and cook for about 4-5 minutes per side. With a slotted spoon, transfer the lamb onto a platter.
4) In the pot, add the onion and cook for about 3-4 minutes. Add the smashed garlic cloves and cook for about 1 minute. Add wine and cook for about 1-2 minutes, scraping up the browned bits from the bottom.
5) Select "Cancel" and stir in the remaining ingredients. Place the leg of lamb in the pot, seam side down.
6) Secure the lid and place the pressure valve to "Seal" position.
7) Select "Manual" and cook under "High Pressure" for about 90 minutes. Select "Cancel" and do a "Natural" release.
8) Remove the lid and place the lamb onto cutting board for about 10 minutes.
9) Through a fine mesh strainer, strain the pot juices and skim any excess fat. Cut the leg of lamb into desired-sized slices and serve alongside pan juices.

Nutrition Information:

Calories per serving: 496; Carbohydrates: 3.8g; Protein: 65g; Fat: 20.5g; Sugar: 1.2g; Sodium: 315mg; Fiber: 0.7g

29 – Garlicky Lamb Shoulder

Serves: 6   Cooking Time: 55 minutes   Preparation Time: 1 minutes

Ingredients:

- 2¼ lb. lamb shoulder without a joint
- 4 garlic cloves, sliced
- 5-6 fresh thyme sprigs, divided
- 1 tbsp. honey
- Salt and freshly ground black pepper, to taste
- 1 C. water
- 3 whole garlic cloves, peeled

Instructions:

1) Season the lamb shoulder with salt and black pepper. Spread 4 thyme sprigs and garlic slices all over the lamb shoulder.
2) Drizzle the lamb shoulder with the honey.
3) Carefully roll the meat together to secure thyme sprigs and garlic slices.
4) Tie the lamb shoulder roll with butcher's strings.
5) In the pot of Instant Pot, place water, whole garlic cloves remaining thyme sprigs. Place the lamb shoulder roll in the water.
6) Secure the lid and place the pressure valve to "Seal" position. Select "Manual" and cook under "High Pressure" for about 40 minutes.
7) Select "Cancel" and do a "Natural" release for about 10 minutes, then do a "Quick" release.
8) Meanwhile, preheat the oven to 430 F. Arrange a rack in the middle of oven. Remove the lid of Instant Pot and transfer lamb shoulder onto a roasting tray.
9) Remove the butcher's string and allow the shoulder to unroll naturally.
10) Then bake the lamb shoulder for about 10-15 minutes or until the meat is browned slightly.
11) Remove from oven and place the lamb shoulder onto a cutting board for about 10 minutes. With a sharp knife, cut the lamb shoulder into desired sized slices and serve.

Nutrition Information:

Calories per serving: 332; Carbohydrates: 4g; Protein: 48g; Fat: 12.5g; Sugar: 2.90g; Sodium: 158mg; Fiber: 0.1g

30 – Spice Marinated Lamb Shanks

Serves: 3   Cooking Time: 56 minutes   Preparation Time: 15 minutes

Ingredients:

For Marinade Mixture:
- ¼ C. olive oil
- 3 garlic cloves, minced
- 2 tbsp. brown sugar
- 1 tbsp. dried oregano
- 1 tbsp. smoked paprika
- ½ tsp. ground cumin
- 1 cinnamon stick

For Lamb Shanks:
- 3 lamb shanks
- ¼ C. olive oil
- 3 carrots, peeled and chopped
- 1 onion, chopped
- 2 bay leaves
- 2 C. red wine
- 4 C. warm beef broth
- 3 tbsp. cornstarch
- 3 tbsp. cold water
- ¼ C. fresh Italian parsley, chopped

Instructions:

1) For marinade: in a large bowl, add all ingredients and mix until well combined.
2) Add lamb shanks and coat with marinade generously.
3) Set aside at room temperature to marinate for at least 30 minutes. Remove the lamb shanks from bowl, reserving any remaining marinade.
4) Place the oil in Instant Pot and select "Sauté". Then add the lamb shanks and cook for about 3-4 minutes per side. With a slotted spoon, transfer the shanks onto a plate.
5) In the pot, add the carrots, onion, bay leaves and reserved marinade and cook for about 4-5 minutes.
6) Stir in the wine and cook for about 10 minutes. Select "Cancel" and place the shanks and broth in the pot.
7) Secure the lid and place the pressure valve to "Seal" position. Select "Manual" and cook under "High Pressure" for about 30 minutes.
8) Select "Cancel" and do a "Natural" release.
9) Remove the lid and with a slotted spoon, transfer the shanks onto a plate. Strain the liquid and return to pot, discarding solids.
10) In a small bowl, dissolve the cornstarch in water. In the pot, add the cornstarch mixture, beating continuously.
11) Select "sauté" and cook for about 2-3 minutes, stirring continuously. Select "Cancel" and pour the sauce over shanks.
12) Serve immediately.

Nutrition Information:
Calories per serving: 965; Carbohydrates: 31.8g; Protein: 88g; Fat: 40g; Sugar: 12.9g; Sodium: 123mg; Fiber: 1.4g

31 - Succulent Lamb Shanks

Serves: 4   Cooking Time: 1 hour 5 minutes   Preparation Time: 15 minutes

Ingredients:

- 4 (10-oz.) lamb shanks
- Salt and freshly ground black pepper, to taste
- 2 tbsp. extra-virgin olive oil
- ½ C. dry white wine
- 1 medium onion, quartered
- 2 garlic cloves, minced
- 1 large carrot, peeled and quartered
- 1 small fennel bulb, quartered, fronds reserved
- 1 bay leaf
- 2¼ C. chicken broth
- 8 oz. dried cannellini beans, soaked for 24 hours, drained and rinsed
- 1 large carrot, peeled and chopped roughly
- 1 medium tomato, seeded and chopped

Instructions:

1) Season the lamb shanks with salt and black pepper. With a piece of foil, cover the shanks and set aside at room temperature for 2 hours.
2) Place the oil in Instant Pot and select "Sauté". Then add the lamb shanks in 2 batches and cook for about 3-4 minutes per side.
3) With a slotted spoon, transfer the shanks onto a plate. In the pot, add the wine and cook for about 3-4 minutes, scraping up the browned bits from the bottom.
4) Select "Cancel" and stir in the shanks, onion, quartered carrot, fennel, garlic and bay leaf.Secure the lid and place the pressure valve to "Seal" position.
5) Select "Manual" and cook under "High Pressure" for about 35 minutes. Select "Cancel" and do a "Natural" release for about 10 minutes, then do a "Quick" release.
6) Remove the lid and with a slotted spoon, transfer the shanks onto a plate. Strain the liquid and return to the pan, discarding the vegetables.
7) Add the beans, chopped carrot and tomato and stir to combine.Secure the lid and place the pressure valve to "Seal" position.
8) Select "Manual" and cook under "High Pressure" for about 10 minutes. Select "Cancel" and do a "Natural" release for about 10 minutes, then do a "Quick" release.
9) Remove the lid and divide the beans mixture into serving bowls.
10) Top each bowl with 1 shank and serve.

Nutrition Information:

Calories per serving: 733; Carbohydrates: 22.2g; Protein: 87g; Fat: 29g; Sugar: 5.4g; Sodium: 889mg; Fiber: 6.8g

32 – Tomato Braised Lamb Shanks

Serves: 4   Cooking Time: 1 hour 5 minutes   Preparation Time: 15 minutes

Ingredients:
- 2 tbsp. olive oil
- 4 (1-lb.) lamb shanks
- Salt and freshly ground black pepper, to taste
- 4 garlic cloves, minced
- ¾ C. dry red wine
- 1 (28-oz.) can crushed tomatoes
- 1 tsp. dried basil
- ¾ tsp. dried oregano
- ¼ C. fresh parsley, chopped

Instructions:
1) Season the lamb shanks with salt and black pepper.
2) Place the oil in Instant Pot and select "Sauté". Then add the lamb shanks in 2 batches and cook for about 3-4 minutes per side.
3) With a slotted spoon, transfer the shanks onto a plate.
4) In the pot, add the garlic and cook for about 1 minute.
5) Add the wine and cook for about 2-3 minutes, scraping up the browned bits from the bottom.
6) Stir in the tomatoes, basil and oregano and cook for about 2 minutes.
7) Select "Cancel" and place the shanks in the pot.
8) Secure the lid and place the pressure valve to "Seal" position.
9) Select "Manual" and cook under "High Pressure" for about 45 minutes.
10) Select "Cancel" and do a "Natural" release.
11) Remove the lid and serve hot.

Nutrition Information:
Calories per serving: 999; Carbohydrates: 18.5g; Protein: 132.9g; Fat: 37.3g; Sugar: 11.5g; Sodium: 724mg; Fiber: 6.7g

33 – Greek Flavoring Meatballs

Serves: 4   Cooking Time: 10 minutes   Preparation Time: 20 minutes

Ingredients:
For Meatballs:
- ¼ C. panko breadcrumbs
- ¼ C. milk
- 1 lb. ground lamb
- 1 tsp. ground coriander
- 1 tsp. ground cumin
- 1 garlic clove, minced
- 1 tsp. dried oregano
- 1 tbsp. fresh mint leaves, chopped
- Salt and freshly ground black pepper, to taste
- ¼ C. feta cheese, crumbled
- 1 tbsp. olive oil

For Salad:
- 1 head butter lettuce, torn into pieces
- 1 large tomato, chopped
- 1 C. mixed olives, pitted
- 1 medium cucumber, thinly sliced
- ¼ C. seeded and diced cucumber
- Salt, to taste
- ½ C. plain Greek yogurt
- 1 garlic clove, minced finely
- 1 tbsp. olive oil
- ¼ tsp. dried dill

For Tzatziki Sauce:

Instructions:
1) For meatballs: in a large bowl, add all the ingredients except for oil and mix until well combined. Make 1-inch balls from the mixture.
2) Arrange the trivet in the bottom of Instant Pot and pour 1 C. of water. Place the meatballs on top of trivet in a single layer.
3) Secure the lid and place the pressure valve to "Seal" position.
4) Select "Manual" and cook under "High Pressure" for about 5 minutes.
5) Select "Cancel" and carefully do a "Quick" release.
6) Remove the lid and transfer the meatballs onto a plate. Remove the water and trivet from pot.
7) With paper towels, pat dry the pot completely. Place the oil in Instant Pot and select "Sauté". Then add the meatballs and cook for about 4-5 minutes or until browned completely.
8) Meanwhile, for salad: in a bowl, mix together all ingredients.
9) For tzatziki sauce: in another bowl, add all the ingredients and mix well.
10) Divide the salad onto serving plates.
11) Select "Cancel" and divide the meatballs onto each plate. Top with tzatziki sauce and serve.

Nutrition Information:
Calories per serving: 425; Carbohydrates: 14.5g; Protein: 37.4g; Fat: 22.6g; Sugar: 6.6g; Sodium: 561mg; Fiber: 2.9g

34 – Abruzzi Style Lamb Pasta

Serves: 6   Cooking Time: 50 minutes   Preparation Time: 15 minutes

Ingredients:

- 1½ lb. lamb loin chops
- 2 tbsp. extra-virgin olive oil
- 1 yellow onion, chopped finely
- 2 garlic cloves, minced
- 1/3 C. dry red wine
- 1 (24-oz.) jar tomato basil sauce
- 1 tbsp. tomato paste
- 1/8 tsp. red pepper flakes
- Salt and freshly ground black pepper, to taste
- ½ C. water
- 1 lb. pappardelle pasta
- 1/3 C. parmesan cheese, shredded

Instructions:

1) Season the lamb chops with salt and black pepper evenly.
2) Place the oil in Instant Pot and select "Sauté". Then add the lamb chops and cook for about 2-3 minutes per side.
3) With a slotted spoon, transfer the lamb chops onto a plate.
4) In the pot, add the onion and garlic and cook for about 4-5 minutes.
5) Add the wine and cook for about 3-4 minutes, scraping up the browned bits from the bottom.
6) Select "Cancel" and stir in the lamb chops, tomato sauce, tomato paste, red pepper flakes, salt and black pepper.
7) Secure the lid and place the pressure valve to "Seal" position.
8) Select "Manual" and cook under "High Pressure" for about 35 minutes.
9) Meanwhile, in a pan of the lightly salted boiling water, cook the pasta for about 8-10 minutes or according to package directions.
10) Drain the pasta for and rinse under cold running water.
11) Divide the pasta onto serving plates.
12) Select "Cancel" of Instant Pot and do a "Natural" release for about 10 minutes, then do a "Quick" release.
13) Remove the lid and place the lab mixture over pasta onto each plate.
14) Top with cheese and serve.

Nutrition Information:

Calories per serving: 536; Carbohydrates: 50.6g; Protein: 44g; Fat: 16.2g; Sugar: 6g; Sodium: 807mg; Fiber: 2.2g

35 - Weekend Dinner Pork Roast

Serves: 8   Cooking Time: 10 minutes   Preparation Time: 50 minutes

Ingredients:

- ¼ C. chicken broth
- ¼ C. fresh lemon juice
- 2 tsp. dried oregano
- 1 tsp. garlic powder
- 1 tsp. onion powder
- Salt and freshly ground black pepper, to taste
- 3 lb. pork roast, cut into 2-3-inch chunks

Instructions:

1) In a bowl, add all the ingredients except for pork pieces and mix well.
2) In the pot of Instant Pot, place the pork pieces and broth mixture and stir to combine.
3) Secure the lid and place the pressure valve to "Seal" position.
4) Select "Manual" and cook under "High Pressure" for about 50 minutes.
5) Select "Cancel" and do a "Natural" release.
6) Remove the lid and with 2 forks, shred the meat.
7) Serve hot.

Nutrition Information:

Calories per serving: 359; Carbohydrates: 0.9g; Protein: 48.8g; Fat: 16.2g; Sugar: 0.4g; Sodium: 140mg; Fiber: 0.2g

38 – Herbed Pork Shoulder

Serves: 14 Cooking Time: 1 hour 5 minutes Preparation Time: 15 minutes

Ingredients:

- 7 lb. boneless pork shoulder, cut into 2 pieces
- 1 tsp. mild paprika
- Salt and freshly ground black pepper, to taste
- 2 C. chicken broth
- 1 C. water
- 1 C. white wine
- 2 C. fresh flat-leaf parsley leaves
- ¼ C. fresh rosemary leaves
- 2 tbsp. fresh thyme leaves
- ¼ C. plus 1 tbsp. extra-virgin olive oil
- 1 large onion, sliced

Instructions:

1) In a large plastic zip bag, place the pork paprika, salt and black pepper.
2) Seal the bag and shake to coat well.
3) Refrigerate to marinate overnight.
4) Place ¼ C. of the oil in the Instant Pot and select "Sauté". Then add 1 piece of pork and sear for about 4-5 minutes per side.
5) Transfer the pork piece onto a plate.
6) Repeat with the remaining pork piece.
7) Select "Cancel" and arrange the trivet in the bottom of Instant Pot.
8) Pour the broth, water and wine in the pot and place the pork pieces on top of trivet.
9) Arrange the onion slices and fresh herbs on top of the roast and drizzle with 1 tbsp. of oil.
10) Secure the lid and place the pressure valve to "Seal" position.
11) Select "Manual" and cook under "High Pressure" for about 45 minutes.
12) Select "Cancel" and do a "Natural" release.
13) Remove the lid and transfer the pork shoulder onto a cutting board.
14) Cut the pork shoulder into desired sized slices and serve.

Nutrition Information:

Calories per serving: 542; Carbohydrates: 4.4g; Protein: 84.8g; Fat: 16.9g; Sugar: 1.1g; Sodium: 359mg; Fiber: 1.6g

36 – Glazed Pork Tenderloin

Serves: 6   Cooking Time: 21 minutes   Preparation Time: 15 minutes

Ingredients:

- 1 C. brown sugar
- 1 C. water
- ½ C. balsamic vinegar
- 4 tbsp. soy sauce
- 2 tsp. dried Italian herb blend
- 1 tsp. garlic powder
- Salt and freshly ground black pepper, to taste
- 2 (1½ lb.) pork tenderloins
- 2 tbsp. olive oil
- 2 tbsp. cornstarch
- 4 tbsp. cold water

Instructions:

1) In a bowl, add the brown sugar, 1 C. of water, vinegar and soy sauce and beat until well combined. Set aside.
2) In a small bowl, mix together the herb blend, garlic powder, salt and black pepper.
3) Season the pork tenderloins with herb mixture evenly.
4) Place the oil in Instant Pot and select "Sauté". Then add the pork tenderloins and cook for about 1-2 minutes per side.
5) Select "Cancel" and place the vinegar mixture on top of pork tenderloins.
6) Secure the lid and place the pressure valve to "Seal" position.
7) Select "Manual" and cook under "High Pressure" for about 15 minutes.
8) Select "Cancel" and do a "Natural" release for about 5 minutes, then do a "Quick" release.
9) Remove the lid and with tongs, transfer the pork loins to a cutting board.
10) Cut the tenderloins into desired sized slices.
11) In a small bowl, dissolve the cornstarch in water.
12) In the pot, add the cornstarch mixture, beating continuously.
13) Select "sauté" and cook for about 1-2 minutes, stirring continuously.
14) Select "Cancel" and pour the glaze over tenderloin slices.
15) Serve immediately.

Nutrition Information:

Calories per serving: 609; Carbohydrates: 27.5g; Protein: 68.5g; Fat: 23.1g; Sugar: 23.8g; Sodium: 782mg; Fiber: 0.2g

37 - Intense Flavored Pork Chops

Serves: 6   Cooking Time: 9 minutes   Preparation Time: 15 minutes

Ingredients:

- 6 boneless pork chops
- 2 tsp. garlic powder
- Salt and freshly ground black pepper, to taste
- 2 tbsp. olive oil
- ½ C. chicken broth
- 1 C. onion, chopped
- 2 medium zucchinis, halved lengthwise and cut crosswise into 1-inch pieces
- 2 C. fresh mushroom, sliced
- 2 (14½-oz.) cans diced tomatoes
- 4 garlic cloves, minced
- 2 tbsp. balsamic vinegar
- 2 tsp. dried Italian seasoning
- 1 bay leaf

Instructions:

1) Season pork chops with garlic powder, salt and black pepper evenly.
2) Place the oil in Instant Pot and select "Sauté". Then add the pork chops and cook for about 2-3 minutes per side.
3) Select "Cancel" and stir in the remaining ingredients.
4) Secure the lid and place the pressure valve to "Seal" position.
5) Select "Manual" and cook under "High Pressure" for about 2-3 minutes.
6) Select "Cancel" and do a "Natural" release.
7) Remove the lid and discard the bay leaf.
8) Serve hot.

Nutrition Information:

Calories per serving: 346; Carbohydrates: 11.7g; Protein: 48.2g; Fat: 11.7g; Sugar: 6.4g; Sodium: 204mg; Fiber: 3.1g

39 – Delicious Weeknight Meal

Serves: 4   Cooking Time: 22 minutes   Preparation Time: 20 minutes

Ingredients:
- ¼ C. extra-virgin olive oil
- 1 lb. lean pork, cut into bite-sized cubes
- 2 potatoes, peeled and quartered
- 2 carrots, peeled and sliced thinly
- 2 celery stalks, sliced thinly
- 2 C. canned crushed tomatoes
- 1 lb. fresh green beans
- 1 large onion, chopped
- Salt and freshly ground black pepper, to taste

Instructions:

1) Place the oil in Instant Pot and select "Sauté". Then add the pork cubes and cook for about 4-5 minutes.
2) Select "Cancel" and stir in the remaining ingredients.
3) Secure the lid and place the pressure valve to "Seal" position.
4) Select "Manual" and cook under "High Pressure" for about 17 minutes.
5) Select "Cancel" and carefully do a "Quick" release.
6) Remove the lid and serve hot.

Nutrition Information:
Calories per serving: 458; Carbohydrates: 41.g; Protein: 37.3g; Fat: 16.9g; Sugar: 13g; Sodium: 386mg; Fiber: 12.1g

40 – Ultra Creamy Pork Ragu

Serves: 8   Cooking Time: 40 minutes   Preparation Time: 15 minutes

Ingredients:

- 3 lb. pork butt roast, trimmed and cut into 4-inch chunks
- Salt and freshly ground black pepper, to taste
- 2 tbsp. olive oil
- 1 large onion, chopped roughly
- 4 large garlic cloves, minced
- 1 C. white wine
- 5 oz. fresh shiitake mushroom, sliced
- 1 oz. dried porcini mushrooms
- 15 fresh thyme stems, tied together with twine
- 3 tbsp. fresh sage, chopped finely
- 1 tbsp. fresh rosemary, chopped finely
- 2½ C. chicken broth
- 3 large carrots, peeled and sliced
- 8 oz. uncooked Rigatoni pasta
- ½ C. Parmesan cheese, grated
- ½ C. heavy cream
- 3 tbsp. fresh parsley, chopped and divided

Instructions:

1) Season the pork chunks with salt and black pepper evenly. Place the oil in Instant Pot and select "Sauté". Then add the pork chunks and cook for 2 minutes per side.
2) With a slotted spoon, transfer the pork chunk onto a plate.
3) In the pot, add the onions and garlic and cook for about 2-3 minutes. Add the wine and cook for about 2 minutes, scraping up the browned bits from the bottom.
4) Select "Cancel" and stir in the cooked pork chunks, mushrooms, herbs, salt, black pepper and broth.
5) Secure the lid and place the pressure valve to "Seal" position. Select "Manual" and cook under "High Pressure" for about 17 minutes.
6) Select "Cancel" and do a "Natural" release. Remove the lid and with a slotted spoon, transfer the pork chunk onto a plate.
7) Remove any fat from the top of mixture. Select "Sauté" and bring the mixture to a boil.
8) Stir in the carrots and pasta and cook for about 10 minutes. Meanwhile, with 2 forks, shred the pork.
9) Select "Cancel" and stir in the shredded meat, Parmesan cheese, cream and 1 tbsp. Of parsley.
10) Serve hot with the garnishing of remaining parsley.

Nutrition Information:

Calories per serving: 587; Carbohydrates: 26.g; Protein: 42g; Fat: 32.7g; Sugar: 3.4g; Sodium: 827mg; Fiber: 2.1g

FISH & SEAFOOD RECIPES

41 – Simplest Frozen Salmon

Serves: 2   Cooking Time: 4 minutes   Preparation Time: 10 minutes

Ingredients:
- 1 C. cold water
- ¼ C. fresh lemon juice
- 2 (5-6-oz.) frozen salmon fillets
- Olive oil cooking spray
- Salt and freshly ground black pepper, to taste

Instructions:

1) Arrange the trivet in the bottom of Instant Pot and pour water and lemon juice.
2) Spray the salmon fillets with cooking spray evenly.
3) Place the salmon fillets on top of trivet in a single layer, skin-side down.
4) Secure the lid and place the pressure valve to "Seal" position.
5) Select "Steam" and just use the default time of 3-4 minutes.
6) Select "Cancel" and carefully do a "Quick" release.
7) Remove the lid and transfer the salmon fillets onto a platter.
8) Sprinkle with salt and black pepper and serve.

Nutrition Information:
Calories per serving: 232; Carbohydrates: 0.6g; Protein: 33.2g; Fat: 10.7g; Sugar: 0.6g; Sodium: 159mg; Fiber: 0.1g

42 – Omega-3 Rich Salmon

Serves: 4   Cooking Time: 5 minutes   Preparation Time: 10 minutes

Ingredients:

- 4 (4-oz.) salmon fillets
- Salt and freshly ground black pepper, to taste
- 1/3 C. fresh parsley, chopped
- 1/3 C. scallions, chopped
- ½ C. canned diced tomatoes with basil, garlic and oregano
- 1 lemon, cut into 4 slices

Instructions:

1) Arrange 4 pieces of foil onto a smooth surface.
2) Season each salmon fillet with salt and black pepper.
3) Place 1 salmon fillet in the center of each foil piece and top each with parsley, followed by scallion, tomatoes and 1 lemon slice
4) Wrap each foil piece around the salmon to secure it.
5) Arrange the trivet in the bottom of Instant Pot and pour 1 C. of water.
6) Place the salmon parcels on top of trivet in a single layer.
7) Secure the lid and place the pressure valve to "Seal" position.
8) Select "Steam" and just use the default time of 5 minutes.
9) Select "Cancel" and carefully do a "Quick" release.
10) Remove the lid and transfer the salmon parcels onto a platter.
11) Carefully, open each parcel and serve.

Nutrition Information:

Calories per serving: 160; Carbohydrates: 2.2g; Protein: 22.5g; Fat: 7.1g; Sugar: 0.9g; Sodium: 94mg; Fiber: 0.8g

43 – Welcoming Salmon Dinner

Serves: 4   Cooking Time: 3 minutes   Preparation Time: 15 minutes

Ingredients:
- ¼ C. olive oil
- 1 tbsp. red wine vinegar
- 1 tbsp. fresh lemon juice
- 1 tbsp. feta cheese, crumbled
- 1 garlic clove, minced
- ¼ tsp. dried oregano
- Salt and freshly ground black pepper, to taste
- 4 (4-oz.) fresh salmon fillets
- 2 fresh rosemary sprigs
- 2 lemon slices

Instructions:

1) For sauce: in a bowl, add the oil, vinegar, lemon juice, feta cheese, garlic, oregano, salt and black pepper and beat until well combined.
2) Season each salmon fillet with a pinch of salt and black pepper.
3) Arrange the trivet in the bottom of Instant Pot and pour 1 C. of water.
4) Arrange the trivet in the bottom of Instant Pot and pour 1 C. of water.
5) Place the salmon fillets on top of trivet in a single layer.
6) Secure the lid and place the pressure valve to "Seal" position.
7) Select "Manual" and cook under "High Pressure" for about 3 minutes.
8) Select "Cancel" and carefully do a "Quick" release.
9) Remove the lid and serve hot.

Nutrition Information:
Calories per serving: 267; Carbohydrates: 0.5g; Protein: 22.4g; Fat: 20.1g; Sugar: 0.2g; Sodium: 116mg; Fiber: 0.1g

44 - Flavor-Packed Cod

Serves: 4   Cooking Time: 8 minutes   Preparation Time: 15 minutes

Ingredients:

- 1 lb. cherry tomatoes, halved
- 2-3 fresh thyme sprigs
- 4 cod fillets
- 1 C. black salt-cured Kalamata olives
- 2 tbsp. pickled capers
- 2 tbsp. olive oil, divided
- 1 garlic clove, pressed
- Salt and freshly ground black pepper, to taste

Instructions:

1) Arrange the steamer basket in the bottom of Instant Pot and pour 2 C. of water.
2) Line the bottom of a heat-proof bowl with some cherry tomatoes, followed by thyme sprigs.
3) Arrange cod fillets on top, followed by the remaining cherry tomatoes, garlic.
4) Drizzle with 1 tbsp. of olive oil and sprinkle with a pinch of salt and black pepper.
5) Place the bowl in steamer basket.
6) Secure the lid and place the pressure valve to "Seal" position.
7) Select "Manual" and cook under "Low Pressure" for about 8 minutes.
8) Select "Cancel" and carefully do a "Quick" release.
9) Remove the lid and divide the cod filets and tomatoes onto the serving plates.
10) Top each fillet with olives and capers and sprinkle with some black pepper.
11) Drizzle with remaining oil and serve.

Nutrition Information:

Calories per serving: 258; Carbohydrates: 7g; Protein: 31.8g; Fat: 12.4g; Sugar: 3g; Sodium: 571mg; Fiber: 2.6g

45 – One-Pot Dinner Cod

Serves: 2   Cooking Time: 5 minutes   Preparation Time: 10 minutes

Ingredients:

- 2 (5-oz.) fresh cod fillets
- ¼ tsp. garlic powder
- Salt and freshly ground black pepper, to taste
- 2 fresh dill sprigs
- 4 lemon slices
- 2 tsp. butter
- 1 C. water

Instructions:

1) Arrange 2 large square sheets of parchment paper onto a smooth surface.
2) Place 1 cod fillet in the center of each parchment paper and sprinkle with garlic powder, salt and black pepper.
3) Top each fillet with dill, followed by lemon slices and butter.
4) Wrap each parchment paper around the cod fillet, leaving space for steam to build.
5) Arrange the trivet in the bottom of Instant Pot and pour 1 C. of water.
6) Place the cod parcels on top of trivet in a single layer.
7) Secure the lid and place the pressure valve to "Seal" position.
8) Select "Manual" and cook under "High Pressure" for about 5 minutes.
9) Select "Cancel" and carefully do a "Quick" release.
10) Remove the lid and transfer the salmon parcels onto a platter.
11) Carefully, open each parcel and serve.

Nutrition Information:

Calories per serving: 151; Carbohydrates: 0.8g; Protein: 25.5g; Fat: 25.5g; Sugar: 0.2g; Sodium: 197mg; Fiber: 0.2g

46 - Terrific Protein Dinner

Serves: 4   Cooking Time: 4 minutes   Preparation Time: 15 minutes

Ingredients:
- 4 (4-oz.) frozen tilapia fillets
- Salt and freshly ground black pepper, to taste
- 3 Roma tomatoes, chopped
- ¼ C. fresh basil, chopped
- 2 garlic cloves, minced
- 2 tbsp. olive oil
- 1 tbsp. balsamic vinegar

Instructions:

1) Season the tilapia fillets with salt and black pepper lightly.
2) Arrange the trivet in the bottom of Instant Pot and pour ½ C. of water.
3) Place the cod parcels on top of trivet in a single layer.
4) Secure the lid and place the pressure valve to "Seal" position.
5) Select "Manual" and cook under "High Pressure" for about 4 minutes.
6) Select "Cancel" and carefully do a "Quick" release.
7) Meanwhile, in a bowl, add the tomatoes, basil, garlic, oil, vinegar, salt and black pepper and toss to coat well.
8) Remove the lid of Instant Pot and transfer the fillets onto serving plates.
9) Top each fillet with tomato mixture and serve.

Nutrition Information:
Calories per serving: 173; Carbohydrates: 4.2g; Protein: 22.1g; Fat: 8.2g; Sugar: 2.5g; Sodium: 84mg; Fiber: 1.2g

47 – Robust Fish Meal

Serves: 4   Cooking Time: 4 minutes   Preparation Time: 15 minutes

Ingredients:

- ¼ C. water
- 4 (4-oz.) frozen sea bass fillets
- 12 cherry tomatoes
- 12-14 black olives
- 2 tbsp. marinated baby capers
- 1/3 C. sliced roasted red peppers
- 2 tbsp. olive oil
- Salt, to taste
- Pinch of red pepper flakes

Instructions:

1) In the pot of Instant Pot, pour the water.
2) Place the fish fillets in water and top with tomatoes, followed by the olives, capers and red peppers.
3) Drizzle with olive oil and sprinkle with salt and red pepper flakes.
4) Secure the lid and place the pressure valve to "Seal" position.
5) Select "Manual" and cook under "High Pressure" for about 4 minutes.
6) Select "Cancel" and do a "Natural" release for about 8 minutes, then do a "Quick" release.
7) Remove the lid and transfer the fish mixture onto serving plates.
8) Serve hot.

Nutrition Information:

Calories per serving: 229; Carbohydrates: 3.8g; Protein: 27.6g; Fat: 11.5g; Sugar: 1.9g; Sodium: 419mg; Fiber: 1.3g

48 - Southern Italian Tuna Pasta

Serves: 4   Cooking Time: 6 minutes   Preparation Time: 15 minutes

Ingredients:

- 12 oz. uncooked penne pasta
- 2 C. cherry tomatoes, halved
- 1/3 C. oil-cured olives, pitted and halved
- 1 small sweet onion, sliced thinly
- 4 garlic cloves, sliced thinly
- 3 tbsp. olive oil
- ¼ tsp. red pepper flakes
- Salt and freshly ground black pepper, to taste
- 2¾ C. water
- 1 (8 oz.) (1½-inch thick) tuna steak
- ½ C. fresh basil leaves, chopped
- 1½ tsp. lemon zest, grated finely
- 2 tbsp. fresh lemon juice

Instructions:

1) In the pot of Instant Pot, add the pasta, tomatoes, olives, onion, olives, garlic, oil, red pepper flakes, salt, black pepper and water and stir to combine.
2) Arrange the tuna steak on top of the pasta mixture.
3) Secure the lid and place the pressure valve to "Seal" position.
4) Select "Manual" and cook under "Low Pressure" for about 6 minutes.
5) Select "Cancel" and carefully do a "Quick" release.
6) Remove the lid and stir in the basil, lemon zest and lemon juice.
7) Break the tuna steak into bite-size chunks and stir with pasta mixture.
8) Set aside for about 5 minutes before serving.

Nutrition Information:

Calories per serving: 483; Carbohydrates: 53.8g; Protein: 28g; Fat: 17.5g; Sugar: 3.4g; Sodium: 194mg; Fiber: 2g

49 – High-Protein Shrimp Meal

Serves: 4   Cooking Time: 2 minutes   Preparation Time: 15 minutes

Ingredients:
- 2 tbsp. butter
- 1 tbsp. garlic
- ½ tsp. red pepper flakes
- 1 (14½-oz) can diced tomatoes
- 1½ C. onions, chopped
- 1 tsp. dried oregano
- Salt, to taste
- 1 lb. frozen raw shrimp, shelled
- 1 C. feta cheese, crumbled
- ½ C. black olives, pitted and sliced
- ¼ C. fresh parsley, chopped

Instructions:

1) Place the butter in Instant Pot and select "Sauté". Then add the garlic and red pepper flakes and cook for about 1 minute.
2) Select "Cancel" and stir in the tomatoes, onions, oregano and salt.
3) Place the shrimp on top and submerge in tomato mixture.
4) Secure the lid and place the pressure valve to "Seal" position.
5) Select "Manual" and cook under "Low Pressure" for about 1 minute.
6) Select "Cancel" and carefully do a "Quick" release.
7) Remove the lid and stir the mixture well.
8) Set the mixture aside to cool slightly.
9) Divide the shrimp mixture onto serving plates and serve with the toppig of feta cheese, olives and parsley.

Nutrition Information:
Calories per serving: 346; Carbohydrates: 13.6g; Protein: 33g; Fat: 17.8g; Sugar: 6.2g; Sodium: 931mg; Fiber: 3.1g

50 – Fancy Shrimp Scampi

Serves: 6   Cooking Time: 0 minute   Preparation Time: 15 minutes

Ingredients:
- ¾ C. dry white wine
- 2 tbsp. olive oil
- 2 tbsp. butter
- 4 tsp. garlic, minced
- ½ tsp. dried oregano
- ½ tsp. red pepper flakes
- 2 lb. frozen raw medium shrimp, peeled and deveined

Instructions:

1) In the pot of Instant Pot, place all the ingredients except for shrimp and mix well.
2) Add the shrimp and stir to combine.
3) Secure the lid and place the pressure valve to "Seal" position.
4) Select "Manual" and cook under "High Pressure" for about 0 minute.
5) Select "Cancel" and carefully do a "Quick" release.
6) Remove the lid and stir the mixture.
7) Serve hot.

Nutrition Information:
Calories per serving: 282; Carbohydrates: 3.9g; Protein: 34.7g; Fat: 11.1g; Sugar: 0.3g; Sodium: 398mg; Fiber: 0.1g

51 – Rustic Shrimp Risotto

Serves: 4   Cooking Time: 12 minutes   Preparation Time: 15 minutes

Ingredients:

- 4 tbsp. unsalted butter
- 1 shallot, chopped
- 2 garlic cloves, chopped finely
- Salt and freshly ground black pepper, to taste
- 1½ C. Arborio rice
- 3 fresh thyme sprigs
- 1/3 C. dry white wine
- 3 C. hot water
- 1 (8-oz.) bottle clam juice
- 1 lb. large shrimp, peeled and deveined
- ½ C. frozen peas
- 2 tbsp. Parmesan cheese, grated
- ½ tsp. lemon zest, grated finely

Instructions:

1) Place 2 tbsp. of the butter in Instant Pot and select "Sauté". Then add the shallot, garlic and a pinch each of salt and pepper and cook for about 3 minutes.
2) Stir in the rice and thyme sprigs and cook for about 3 minutes.
3) Stir in the wine and cook for, about 1 minute.
4) Select "Cancel" and stir in the hot water and clam juice.
5) Secure the lid and place the pressure valve to "Seal" position.
6) Select "Manual" and cook under "High Pressure" for about 5 minutes.
7) Select "Cancel" and carefully do a "Quick" release.
8) Meanwhile, season the shrimp with salt and black pepper.
9) Remove the lid and immediately, stir in the shrimp and peas.
10) Immediately, secure the lid for about 5 minutes.
11) Remove the lid and stir in the remaining butter, Parmesan cheese and lemon zest.
12) Discard the thyme sprigs and serve.

Nutrition Information:

Calories per serving: 525; Carbohydrates: 69.7g; Protein: 28.7g; Fat: 12.8g; Sugar: 3g; Sodium: 31mg; Fiber: 3.3g

52 – Richly Creamy Shrimp Spaghetti

Serves: 6   Cooking Time: 5 minutes   Preparation Time: 15 minutes

Ingredients:
- 1 tbsp. butter
- 6 garlic cloves, minced
- 3¾ C. chicken broth
- 1 lb. thin spaghetti, broken
- 1 lb. raw jumbo shrimp, peeled and deveined
- 8 oz. fresh spinach
- 2 C. Parmesan cheese, shredded
- 1½ C. warm heavy cream
- 6 tbsp. fresh lemon juice
- 1-2 tsp. lemon zest, grated
- Salt and freshly ground black pepper, to taste

Instructions:

1) Place the butter in Instant Pot and select "Sauté". Then add the garlic and cook for about 1 minute.
2) Stir in the broth and cook for about 1 minute.
3) Select "Cancel" and place the spaghetti in broth.
4) Secure the lid and place the pressure valve to "Seal" position.
5) Select "Manual" and cook under "High Pressure" for about 3 minutes.
6) Select "Cancel" and carefully do a "Quick" release.
7) Remove the lid and immediately, stir in the remaining ingredients.
8) Immediately, secure the lid for about 3-5 minutes.
9) Remove the lid and serve hot.

Nutrition Information:
Calories per serving: 80; Carbohydrates: 47.6g; Protein: 40.9g; Fat: 24.5g; Sugar: 1g; Sodium: 1219mg; Fiber: 1g

53 – Amazing Shrimp Pasta

Serves: 4   Cooking Time: 8 minutes   Preparation Time: 15 minutes

Ingredients:

- 2 tbsp. butter
- 1 tbsp. olive oil
- ½ C. onion, chopped
- 2 garlic cloves, chopped
- 1/8 tsp. red pepper flakes
- ¾ lb. shrimp, peeled and deveined
- 8 oz. penne pasta
- 1½ C. marinara sauce
- 1 C. heavy cream
- ¾ C. water
- Salt and freshly ground black pepper, to taste
- ½ C. fresh basil, chopped

Instructions:

1) Place the butter and oil in Instant Pot and select "Sauté". Then add the onion, garlic and red pepper flakes and cook for about 2-3 minutes.
2) Select "Cancel" and stir in the remaining ingredients except for basil.
3) Secure the lid and place the pressure valve to "Seal" position.
4) Select "Manual" and cook under "High Pressure" for about 5 minutes.
5) Select "Cancel" and carefully do a "Quick" release.
6) Remove the lid and stir in the basil.
7) Set aside for about 2-3 minutes before serving.

Nutrition Information:

Calories per serving: 539; Carbohydrates: 48g; Protein: 28.5g; Fat: 25.7g; Sugar:9; Sodium: 700mg; Fiber: 2.9g

54 – Mussels

Serves: 2   Cooking Time: 3 minutes   Preparation Time: 15 minutes

Ingredients:
- 2 tbsp. unsalted butter
- 2 tbsp. olive oil
- 1 lb. mussels, cleaned and de-bearded
- 3 garlic cloves, minced
- 1 shallot, minced
- 3-4 tbsp. fresh parsley, chopped
- 2-3 scallions, chopped
- ¼ C. white wine
- 1 C. chicken broth
- Salt and freshly ground black pepper, to taste

Instructions:

1) Place the butter and oil in Instant Pot and select "Sauté". Then add the shallots and cook for about 2 minutes.
2) Add the garlic and cook for about 1 minute.
3) Stir in the wine and cook down for about 1 minute.
4) Select "Cancel" and stir in the broth, half of the parsley and scallions.
5) Place the mussels and gently, submerge in the broth.
6) Secure the lid and place the pressure valve to "Seal" position.
7) Select "Manual" and cook under "High Pressure" for about 3 minutes.
8) Select "Cancel" and carefully do a "Quick" release.
9) Remove the lid and transfer the mussels into a bowl.
10) Garnish with remaining parsley and scallions and serve.

Nutrition Information:
Calories per serving: 480; Carbohydrates: 13.9g; Protein: 30.5g; Fat: 31.4g; Sugar: 1g; Sodium: 1190mg; Fiber: 0.7g

55 – Super-Simple Octopus

Serves: 4   Cooking Time: 15 minutes   Preparation Time: 15 minutes

Ingredients:
- 2 lb. octopus, cleaned
- 1 C. water
- 1 lemon, sliced
- 2 tbsp. olive oil

Instructions:

1) In the pot of Instant Pot, place water, octopus and half of the lemon slices.
2) Secure the lid and place the pressure valve to "Seal" position.
3) Select "Manual" and cook under "High Pressure" for about 15 minutes.
4) Select "Cancel" and carefully do a "Quick" release.
5) Remove the lid and drain the octopus.
6) Transfer the octopus onto a platter.
7) Cut the octopus into strips, discarding the hard beak in the center of octopus body.
8) In a large bowl, add the octopus pieces and oil and toss to coat well.
9) Serve immediately.

Nutrition Information:
Calories per serving: 435; Carbohydrates: 11g; Protein: 66.8g; Fat: 12.4g; Sugar: 0.1g; Sodium: 1000mg; Fiber: 0.1g

VEGETARIAN & VEGAN RECIPES

56 – Spring Side Dish

Serves: 5   Cooking Time: 2 minutes   Preparation Time: 10 minutes

Ingredients:
- 1 C. cold water
- 1½ lb. asparagus, trimmed
- 1 garlic clove, minced
- 1 tsp. lemon zest
- 3 tbsp. olive oil
- 1 tbsp. fresh lemon juice
- Salt and freshly ground black pepper, to taste

Instructions:

1) Arrange the trivet in the bottom of Instant Pot and pour water.
2) Place the asparagus spears on top of trivet.
3) Select "Steam" and just use the default time of 0 minute.
4) Select "Cancel" and carefully do a "Quick" release.
5) Remove the lid and transfer the asparagus into a bowl.
6) Remove the trivet and water from pot.
7) With paper towels, pat dry the pot.
8) Place the oil in Instant Pot and select "Sauté". Then add the garlic and lemon zest and cook for about 1 minute.
9) Add the cooked asparagus, lemon juice, salt and black pepper and cook for about 1 minute.
10) Select "Cancel" and serve immediately.

Nutrition Information:
Calories per serving: 101; Carbohydrates: 5.6g; Protein: 3.1g; Fat: 8.6g; Sugar: 2.7g; Sodium: 34mg; Fiber: 2.9g

57 – High-Carb Luncheon

Serves: 4   Cooking Time: 15 minutes   Preparation Time: 15 minutes

Ingredients:

- 14 oz. fresh spinach, chopped
- 4 medium potatoes, cut in large pieces
- 1 C. water
- ¼ C. extra-virgin olive oil
- 2 tbsp. fresh lemon juice
- 4 garlic cloves, chopped
- Salt and freshly ground black pepper, to taste

Instructions:

1) In the pot of Instant Pot, place all the ingredients and stir to combine.
2) Secure the lid and place the pressure valve to "Seal" position.
3) Select "Manual" and cook under "High Pressure" for about 15 minutes.
4) Select "Cancel" and carefully do a "Quick" release.
5) Remove the lid and serve.

Nutrition Information:

Calories per serving: 284; Carbohydrates: 38.2g; Protein: 6.7g; Fat: 13.3g; Sugar: 3.1g; Sodium: 134mg; Fiber: 7.4g

58 - 3-Veggies Combo

Serves: 6   Cooking Time: 17 minutes   Preparation Time: 20 minutes

Ingredients:
- ½ C. extra-virgin olive oil
- 2 potatoes, quartered
- 1 lb. fresh green beans, trimmed
- 1 large zucchini, quartered
- 1½ onion, sliced thinly
- 1 (15-oz.) can diced tomatoes
- 1 bunch fresh dill, chopped
- ½ bunch fresh parsley, chopped
- 1 tsp. dried oregano
- Salt and freshly ground black pepper, to taste
- 1 C. water

Instructions:

1) Place the oil in Instant Pot and select "Sauté". Then add all the vegetables and cook for about 1-2 minutes.
2) Select "Cancel" and stir in the remaining ingredients.
3) Secure the lid and place the pressure valve to "Seal" position.
4) Select "Manual" and cook under "High Pressure" for about 15 minutes.
5) Select "Cancel" and carefully do a "Quick" release.
6) Remove the lid and serve hot.

Nutrition Information:
Calories per serving: 251; Carbohydrates: 24.1g; Protein: 4.3g; Fat: 17.3g; Sugar: 5.9g; Sodium: 47mg; Fiber: 6.5g

59 – Winner Stuffed Acorn Squash

Serves: 6   Cooking Time: 25 minutes   Preparation Time: 20 minutes

Ingredients:

- ½ C. uncooked wild rice
- 1¾ C. water
- Salt, to taste
- 3 (1-lb.) acorn squashes, halved lengthwise, stems trimmed and seeded
- 1 tbsp. olive oil
- ½ of small yellow onion, chopped finely
- 1 tbsp. garlic, minced
- 8 oz. fresh mushrooms, chopped finely
- ½ tsp. freshly ground black pepper
- 1 (15-oz.) can low-sodium chickpeas, rinsed and drained
- 1/3 C. low-sugar dried cranberries
- ¼ C. pecans, chopped
- 1 tbsp. fresh thyme leaves, chopped

Instructions:

1) In the pot of Instant Pot, place rice, water and a pinch of salt.
2) Secure the lid and place the pressure valve to "Seal" position.
3) Select "Manual" and cook under "High Pressure" for about 15 minutes.
4) Select "Cancel" and do a "Natural" release.
5) Remove the lid and transfer the rice into a bowl.
6) With paper towels, pat dry the pot.
7) Arrange the steamer basket in the bottom of Instant Pot and pour ½ C. of water.
8) Place the squash halves in steamer basket, cut sides up.
9) Secure the lid and place the pressure valve to "Seal" position.
10) Select "Manual" and cook under "High Pressure" for about 4 minutes.
11) Remove the lid and arrange the squash halves on a large serving plate.
12) Select "Cancel" and do a "Natural" release for about 5 minutes, then do a "Quick" release.
13) Meanwhile, heat the olive oil in a large skillet over medium heat and sauté the onion for about 4 minutes.
14) Add the garlic and sauté for about 1 minute.
15) Add the mushrooms, salt and black pepper and cook for about 5-7 minutes.
16) Stir in the chickpeas, cranberries, pecans, thyme and cooked rice and cook for about 2 minutes.
17) Spoon the hot filling into each squash half and serve immediately.

Nutrition Information:

Calories per serving: 473; Carbohydrates: 80.6g; Protein: 19.5g; Fat: 11.2g; Sugar: 9.3g; Sodium: 55mg; Fiber: 18.1g

60 – Savory Herbed Quinoa

Serves: 6   Cooking Time: 14 minutes   Preparation Time: 10 minutes

Ingredients:

- 2 C. quinoa, soaked for 1 hour, rinsed and drained
- 1 tbsp. avocado oil
- 1 onion, chopped
- 1 tsp. garlic, minced
- 2½ C. vegetable broth
- Salt and freshly ground black pepper, to taste
- 1 tbsp. lemon zest
- 1 tsp. dried rosemary
- 1 tsp. dried oregano
- 1 tsp. dried marjoram

Instructions:

1) Place the oil in Instant Pot and select "Sauté". Then add the onion and cook for about 8 minutes.
2) Add the quinoa and garlic and cook for about 5 minutes, stirring occasionally.
3) Select "Cancel" and stir in the broth, salt and black pepper.
4) Secure the lid and place the pressure valve to "Seal" position.
5) Select "Manual" and cook under "High Pressure" for about 1 minute.
6) Select "Cancel" and do a "Natural" release for about 10 minutes, then do a "Quick" release.
7) Remove the lid and with a fork, fluff the quinoa.
8) Serve warm.

Nutrition Information:

Calories per serving: 238; Carbohydrates: 39.3g; Protein: 10.4g; Fat: 4.4g; Sugar: 1.1g; Sodium: 349mg; Fiber: 4.8g

61 - Bold Flavors Loaded Meal

Serves: 4   Cooking Time: 1 minute   Preparation Time: 15 minutes

Ingredients:

- 1½ C. low-sodium vegetable broth
- 1 C. quinoa, rinsed
- 1 C. fresh shiitake mushroom, sliced
- ½ C. carrots, peeled and shredded
- ½ C. cherry tomatoes, halved
- ¼ C. hemp seeds, shelled
- ¼ C. red onion, thinly sliced
- ¼ C. black olives, pitted and chopped
- 1 handful fresh spinach
- 1 tbsp. olive oil
- Salt and freshly ground black pepper, to taste

Instructions:

1) In the pot of Instant Pot, place the broth, quinoa and mushrooms and stir to combine.
2) Secure the lid and place the pressure valve to "Seal" position.
3) Select "Manual" and cook under "High Pressure" for about 1 minute.
4) Select "Cancel" and do a "Natural" release.
5) Remove the lid and stir in the remaining ingredients.
6) Set aside, covered for about 5 minutes before serving.

Nutrition Information:

Calories per serving: 241; Carbohydrates: 36.4g; Protein: 8.3g; Fat: 7.6g; Sugar: 3g; Sodium: 244mg; Fiber: 5g

62 – Plant-Based Dinner

Serves: 4   Cooking Time: 3 minutes   Preparation Time: 20 minutes

Ingredients:

- 1 C. French green lentils, soaked overnight and drained
- 1 C. pearl couscous
- 2 carrots, peeled and chopped
- 2 red bell peppers, seeded and chopped
- 1 medium yellow onion, chopped
- 6 garlic cloves, minced
- 2-3 fresh thyme sprigs
- 2 bay leaves
- 3½ C. low-sodium vegetable broth
- Salt and freshly ground black pepper, to taste
- 2 C. cherry tomatoes, quartered
- 15 green olives, pitted and sliced
- 1 C. fresh dill, chopped finely
- 1 C. fresh parsley, chopped finely
- 2½ tbsp. extra-virgin olive oil
- 1½ tbsp. red wine vinegar

Instructions:

1) In the pot of Instant Pot, place lentils, couscous, carrots, bell peppers, onion, garlic, thyme sprigs, bay leaves, broth, salt and black pepper and stir to combine.
2) Secure the lid and place the pressure valve to "Seal" position.
3) Select "Manual" and cook under "High Pressure" for about 3 minutes.
4) Select "Cancel" and do a "Natural" release for about 10 minutes, then do a "Quick" release.
5) Remove the lid and discard the thyme sprigs and bay leaves.
6) Transfer the lentil mixture to a large bowl and let it come to room temperature.
7) Add the remaining ingredients and stir to combine.
8) Serve immediately.

Nutrition Information:

Calories per serving: 538; Carbohydrates: 86.1g; Protein: 24.7g; Fat: 12.4g; Sugar: 9.2g; Sodium: 309mg; Fiber: 20.6g

63 – Vegan-Friendly Bolognese

Serves: 4   Cooking Time: 20 minutes   Preparation Time: 15 minutes

Ingredients:

- 7 oz. fresh button mushrooms, chopped finely
- 2 tbsp. olive oil
- 1 medium onion, chopped finely
- 1 large carrot, peeled and chopped finely
- 1 large celery stalk, chopped finely
- Salt, to taste
- 1 C. dry red lentils, soaked for 15-20 minutes and rinsed
- 2 C. tomato passata
- 10 black olives, chopped roughly
- 2 dates, pitted and chopped roughly
- 3 garlic cloves, chopped finely
- 1 tsp. paprika
- ½ tsp. red pepper flakes
- 1 vegetable stock cube
- 2 tbsp. low-sodium soy sauce
- 1 tbsp. balsamic vinegar
- 2/3 C. water

Instructions:

1) Place the oil in Instant Pot and select "Sauté". Then add the onions, carrot, celery and salt and cook for about 7-8 minutes.
2) Select "Cancel" and stir in the remaining ingredients.
3) Secure the lid and place the pressure valve to "Seal" position.
4) Select "Manual" and cook under "High Pressure" for about 12 minutes.
5) Select "Cancel" and do a "Natural" release.
6) Remove the lid and stir the mixture well.
7) Serve hot.

Nutrition Information:

Calories per serving: 342; Carbohydrates: 2g; Protein: 17.5g; Fat: 9.4g; Sugar: 13.2g; Sodium: 634mg; Fiber: 19.6g

64 – Summery Luncheon Chickpeas

Serves: 6   Cooking Time: 45 minutes   Preparation Time: 15 minutes

Ingredients:
For Chickpeas:
- 1½ C. dried chickpeas
- 4 C. vegetable broth

For Salsa:
- A handful of fresh parsley
- A handful of fresh basil
- 2 tbsp. marinated capers
- 2 garlic cloves
- 2½ tbsp. fresh lemon juice
- Salt, to taste
- ¼ C. olive oil
- ¼ tsp. honey

Instructions:

1) In the pot of Instant Pot, place the chickpeas and broth.
2) Secure the lid and place the pressure valve to "Seal" position.
3) Select "Manual" and cook under "High Pressure" for about 45 minutes.
4) Meanwhile, for salsa: in a food processor, add all the ingredients and pulse until fairly smooth.
5) Transfer the salsa into a bowl and set aside.
6) Select "Cancel" and do a "Natural" release for about 5 minutes, then do a "Quick" release.
7) Remove the lid and divide the chickpeas onto serving plates.
8) Top with salsa and serve.

Nutrition Information:
Calories per serving: 286; Carbohydrates: 32.2g; Protein: 13.3g; Fat: 12.5g; Sugar: 6.3g; Sodium: 637mg; Fiber: 9g

65 – Uniquely Tasty Beans

Serves: 8   Cooking Time: 20 minutes   Preparation Time: 15 minutes

Ingredients:

- 3 C. dried lima beans
- 8 C. water
- Salt, to taste
- ¼ C. plus 2 tbsp. extra-virgin olive oil
- 1 large yellow onion, chopped finely
- 1 celery stalk, chopped finely
- 1 garlic clove, peeled
- 1 (28-oz.) can crushed tomatoes
- 1 tsp. dried oregano
- Freshly ground black pepper, to taste
- ½ C. feta cheese, crumbled
- ¼ C. fresh parsley, chopped

Instructions:

1) In the pot of Instant Pot, place the beans, water, and salt.
2) Leave the pot aside to let the beans soak for 10-12 hours.
3) Secure the lid and place the pressure valve to "Seal" position.
4) Select "Manual" and cook under "High Pressure" for about 15 minutes.
5) Select "Cancel" and do a "Natural" release for about 10 minutes, then do a "Quick" release.
6) Remove the lid and drain the beans, reserving 1 C. of the cooking liquid into a bowl.
7) With paper towels, pat dry the pot.
8) Place ¼ C. of the oil in Instant Pot and select "Sauté". Then add the onion, celery and garlic and cook for about 5 minutes.
9) Select "Cancel" and stir in the beans, reserved cooking liquid, tomatoes, oregano, salt and black pepper.
10) Secure the lid and place the pressure valve to "Seal" position.
11) Select "Bean/Chili" and just use the default time of 5 minutes.
12) Select "Cancel" and do a "Natural" release for about 15 minutes, then do a "Quick" release.
13) Remove the lid and transfer the beans mixture into a bowl.
10) Top with the seta and parsley.
11) Drizzle with remaining oil and serve.

Nutrition Information:

Calories per serving: 208; Carbohydrates: 18.2g; Protein: 6.5g; Fat: 13.3g; Sugar: 4.7g; Sodium: 144mg; Fiber: 4.6g

66 - Green Garden Risotto

Serves: 4   Cooking Time: 9 minutes   Preparation Time: 15 minutes

Ingredients:
For Risotto:
- ½ of large onion, chopped finely
- 1 celery stalk, chopped finely
- 2 tbsp. olive oil
- Salt, to taste
- 2 large garlic cloves, chopped finely
- ½ of jalapeño pepper, chopped

- 1¼ C. Arborio rice
- 1 C. fresh spinach, chopped
- 1 zucchini, cubed
- 1½ C. frozen peas
- 3 C. vegetable broth
- Pinch of freshly ground black pepper

For Finishing:
- 1 tsp. lemon zest, grated
- 2 tbsp. fresh lemon juice

- 2 tbsp. nutritional yeast flakes
- 1 tsp. miso paste

Instructions:

1) For risotto: place the oil in Instant Pot and select "Sauté". Then add the onions, celery and salt and cook for about 3-4 minutes.
2) Select "Cancel" and stir in the remaining ingredients.
3) Secure the lid and place the pressure valve to "Seal" position.
4) Select "Manual" and cook under "High Pressure" for about 5 minutes.
5) Select "Cancel" and do a "Natural" release for about 5 minutes, then do a "Quick" release.
6) Remove the lid and lemon zest, lemon juice, nutritional yeast and miso paste.
7) Serve hot.

Nutrition Information:
Calories per serving: 393; Carbohydrates: 63.8g; Protein: 14.4g; Fat: 9.1g; Sugar: 5.4g; Sodium: 732mg; Fiber: 7.6g

67 – Italian Style Mac n' Cheese

Serves: 6   Cooking Time: 6 minutes   Preparation Time: 15 minutes

Ingredients:

- 17 oz. elbow macaroni
- 2 tbsp. butter
- 2 garlic cloves, chopped finely
- 1¼ C. tomato passata, divided
- ½ tsp. red pepper flakes
- Salt, to taste
- 4 C. water
- 1 C. marinated artichoke hearts, chopped roughly
- 10-12 black olives, sliced
- ½ C. sun-dried tomatoes, sliced
- 1 C. almond milk
- 1 C. cheddar cheese, grated
- ½ C. mozzarella cheese, grated
- ¼-½ C. Parmesan cheese, grated
- ¼ C. scallions, chopped

Instructions:

1) In the pot of Instant Pot, place the macaroni, butter, garlic, 1 C. of tomato passata, red pepper flakes, salt and water and stir to combine.
2) Secure the lid and place the pressure valve to "Seal" position.
3) Select "Manual" and cook under "High Pressure" for about 4 minutes.
4) Select "Cancel" and do a "Natural" release for about 5 minutes, then do a "Quick" release.
5) Remove the lid and stir in the artichokes, olives, sun-dried tomatoes, milk, remaining tomato passata and half of all the cheeses.
6) Select "Sauté" and cook for about 1 minute, stirring continuously.
7) Stir in the remaining cheeses and cook for about 30-60 seconds, stirring continuously.
8) Select "Cancel" and serve hot with the garnishing of scallion.

Nutrition Information:

Calories per serving: 638; Carbohydrates: 74.3g; Protein: 27.2g; Fat: 27.6g; Sugar: 7g; Sodium: 823mg; Fiber: 7.1g

68 – Light Pasta Meal

Serves: 4   Cooking Time: 3 minutes   Preparation Time: 15 minutes

Ingredients:
For Pasta:
- 4 C. water
- 10 oz. spiral pasta
- 2 C. fresh baby spinach leaves
- 5 cherry tomatoes, quartered

- 1 garlic clove, chopped finely
- 1 tsp. lemon zest, grated
- Salt, to taste

For Finishing:
- 1 tbsp. fresh lemon juice
- 1 tbsp. olive oil
- ½ C. ricotta cheese
- 1/3 C. Parmesan cheese, grated
- 3-4 fresh basil leaves, chopped

- 6-8 cherry tomatoes, quartered
- 1 garlic clove, chopped finely
- 1 tsp. lemon zest, grated
- Salt and freshly ground black pepper, to taste

Instructions:

1) For pasta: in the pot of Instant Pot, place all the ingredients and stir to combine.
2) Secure the lid and place the pressure valve to "Seal" position.
3) Select "Manual" and cook under "High Pressure" for about 3 minutes.
4) Select "Cancel" and carefully do a "Quick" release.
5) Remove the lid and stir in the remaining ingredients until well cobined.
6) Serve immediately.

Nutrition Information:
Calories per serving: 372; Carbohydrates: 44.8g; Protein: 20.5g; Fat: 13.1g; Sugar: 1.5g; Sodium: 625mg; Fiber: 1g

69 – Best-Ever Hummus

Serves: 10   Cooking Time: 25 minutes   Preparation Time: 5 minutes

Ingredients:

- 3 C. water
- 8 oz. dried chickpeas, soaked in salted water overnight and drained
- 1 garlic clove, peeled
- ½ C. tahini
- 2 tbsp. fresh lemon juice
- 1 tsp. kosher salt
- 1-2 tbsp. olive oil
- Za'atar, to taste

Instructions:

1) In the pot of Instant Pot, place water, chickpeas and garlic.
2) Secure the lid and place the pressure valve to "Seal" position.
3) Select "Manual" and cook under "High Pressure" for about 25 minutes.
4) Select "Cancel" and do a "Natural" release.
5) Remove the lid and drain the chickpeas, reserving 1 C. of the cooking liquid.
6) In a food processor, add the chickpeas, tahini, lemon juice and salt and pulse until mostly smooth.
7) While the motor is running, add about ½ C. of the reserved cooking liquid and pulse until smooth.
8) Transfer the hummus into a serving bowl and drizzle with olive oil.
9) Sprinkle with za'atar and serve.

Nutrition Information:

Calories per serving: 167; Carbohydrates: 16.5g; Protein: 6.5g; Fat: 9.2g; Sugar: 2.6g; Sodium: 255mg; Fiber: 5.1g

70 - Cheese-Free Queso

Serves: 8   Cooking Time: 5 minutes   Preparation Time: 15 minutes

Ingredients:

- 1 C. water
- 2 C. cauliflower florets
- ¾ C. carrot, cut into thick coins
- ¼ C. raw cashews
- 1 (10-oz.) can diced tomatoes with green chiles
- ¼ C. nutritional yeast
- ½ tsp. smoked paprika
- ¼ tsp. red chili powder
- 1/8 tsp. mustard powder
- Salt, to taste
- ½ C. bell pepper, seeded and chopped
- 2 tbsp. red onion, minced
- ¼ C. fresh cilantro, minced

Instructions:

1) In the pot of Instant Pot, place the water, cauliflower, carrots and cashews.
2) Secure the lid and place the pressure valve to "Seal" position.
3) Select "Manual" and cook under "High Pressure" for about 5 minutes.
4) Select "Cancel" and carefully do a "Quick" release.
5) Remove the lid and drain the extra water from veggie mixture.
6) Drain the can of tomatoes, reserving the juices into a bowl.
7) In a blender, add the drained veggie mixture, reserved tomato juices, nutritional yeast, smoked paprika, chili powder, mustard powder and salt and pulse until smooth.
8) Transfer the mixture into a bowl and stir in the canned tomatoes and green chiles, bell pepper, onion and cilantro.
9) Serve immediately.

Nutrition Information:

Calories per serving: 63; Carbohydrates: 8.4g; Protein: 4g; Fat: 2.4g; Sugar: 2.8g; Sodium: 42mg; Fiber: 3g

SOUPS & STEWS RECIPES

71 – Immunity Boosting Chicken Soup

Serves: 4   Cooking Time: 23 minutes   Preparation Time: 15 minutes

Ingredients:

For Spices Mixture:
- 2 tsp. Italian seasoning
- 1 tsp. turmeric
- ½ tsp. garlic powder
- ¼ tsp. ground ginger
- ¼ tsp. cayenne pepper

For Soup:
- 1 lb. boneless, skinless chicken breasts, cut into cubes
- Salt and freshly ground black pepper, to taste
- 1 tbsp. olive oil
- ½ of small yellow onion, sliced thinly
- 2 celery stalks, sliced
- 8 oz. baby carrots, halved
- 12 oz. frozen cauliflower rice
- 8-12 oz. frozen chopped sweet potato
- 4 C. chicken broth

Instructions:

1) For spice mixture: I a bowl, mix together all ingredients. Set aside.
2) Season the chicken cubes with salt and black pepper evenly.
3) Place the oil in Instant Pot and select "Sauté". Then add the onion and cook for about 2-3 minutes.
4) Add the chicken cubes and cook for about 4-5 minutes. Add the spices and stir to combine.
5) Select "Cancel" and stir in the remaining ingredients. Secure the lid and place the pressure valve to "Seal" position.
6) Select "Manual" and cook under "High Pressure" for about 15 minutes.
7) Select "Cancel" and carefully do a "Quick" release. Remove the lid and serve hot.

Nutrition Information:
Calories per serving: 392; Carbohydrates: 23.9g; Protein: 41.9g; Fat: 14.3g; Sugar: 9.9g; Sodium: 998mg; Fiber: 6.2g

72 – Classic Wedding Soup

Serves: 10   Cooking Time: 10 minutes   Preparation Time: 20 minutes

Ingredients:
For Meatballs:
- ½ lb. ground chicken sausage
- ½ lb. ground turkey
- ½ C. Parmesan cheese, grated
- ¼ C. milk
- 1 egg
- 1 white bread slice, torn
- 3 tsp. Italian seasoning
- Salt and freshly ground black pepper, to taste
- ½ tsp. garlic powder

For Soup:
- 2 tbsp. extra-virgin olive oil
- 3 carrots, peeled and chopped
- 2 celery stalks, chopped
- 1 medium onion, chopped
- 3 garlic cloves, minced
- 9 C. low-sodium chicken broth
- 1 tsp. dried dill
- Salt and freshly ground black pepper, to taste
- ¾ C. pastina
- 10 oz. fresh baby spinach

Instructions:

1) For meatballs: in a large bowl, add all ingredients and with your hands, mix until well combined. Make 1-inch meatballs from the mixture.
2) Place the oil in Instant Pot and select "Sauté". Then add the carrots, celery and onion and cook for about 5-6 minutes.
3) Add the garlic and cook for about 1 minute. Select "Cancel" and stir in the broth, dill, salt and black pepper.
4) Carefully, place the meatballs in broth mixture, followed by the pastina. Secure the lid and place the pressure valve to "Seal" position.
5) Select "Manual" and cook under "High Pressure" for about 3 minutes.
6) Select "Cancel" and do a "Natural" release for about 15 minutes, then do a "Quick" release. Remove the lid and stir in the spinach.
7) Set the soup aside for about 5 minutes before serving.

Nutrition Information:
Calories per serving: 256; Carbohydrates: 21.9g; Protein: 18.8g; Fat: 10.6g; Sugar: 2g; Sodium: 312mg; Fiber: 1.4g

73 – Hearty Pasta e Fagioli Soup

Serves: 8   Cooking Time: 27 minutes   Preparation Time: 15 minutes

Ingredients:

- 1 tbsp. olive oil
- 2 celery stalks, sliced thinly
- 2 C. carrot, peeled and chopped
- 1 large yellow onion, chopped
- 4 garlic cloves, minced
- 1½ lb. ground beef
- 2 tsp. chili powder
- 1 (14½-oz.) can diced tomatoes
- 1 (15-oz.) can great northern white beans, rinsed and drained
- 1 (15-oz.) can red kidney beans, rinsed and drained
- 5 oz. uncooked elbow macaroni
- 1 (14½-oz.) can tomato sauce
- 5 C. chicken broth
- Salt and freshly ground black pepper, to taste
- ½ C. Parmesan cheese, grated

Instructions:

1) Place the oil in Instant Pot and select "Sauté". Then add the carrot, celery and onion and cook for about 4-5 minutes.
2) Add the garlic and cook for about 1 minute.
3) Add the ground beef and cook for about 6-8 minutes.
4) Drain the grease from pot.
5) Stir in the chili powder and cook for about 1 minute.
6) Add the tomatoes and cook for about 6-8 minutes.
7) Select "Cancel" and stir in the beans, pasta, tomato sauce and broth.
8) Secure the lid and place the pressure valve to "Seal" position.
9) Select "Manual" and cook under "High Pressure" for about 4 minutes.
10) Select "Cancel" and do a "Natural" release for about 5 minutes, then do a "Quick" release.
11) Remove the lid and serve with the topping of cheese.

Nutrition Information:

Calories per serving: 448; Carbohydrates: 46.3g; Protein: 42g; Fat: 10.4g; Sugar:7.9g; Sodium: 1203mg; Fiber: 11.8g

74 - Rustic Tortellini Soup

Serves: 8   Cooking Time: 21 minutes   Preparation Time: 5 minutes

Ingredients:
- 1 lb. ground Italian sausage
- 1 medium white onion, chopped
- 2 garlic cloves, minced
- 1 (10-oz.) package frozen cheese tortellini
- 1 large carrot, peeled and cut into ¼-inch rounds
- 1 (14-oz.) can petite diced tomatoes with juice
- 2 (8-oz.) cans tomato sauce
- 6 C. beef broth
- 1 bay leaf
- ½ tsp. dried basil
- ½ tsp. dried oregano
- 1 medium zucchini, chopped
- 1 medium green bell pepper, seeded and chopped

Instructions:

1) Place the oil in Instant Pot and select "Sauté". Then add the ground sausage and cook for about 8-10 minutes, breaking up with a wooden spoon.
2) Drain off any excess grease from the pot.
3) Add the onion and garlic and cook for about 4-5 minutes.
4) Select "Cancel" and stir in the tortellini, carrot, tomatoes, tomato sauce, broth, basil and oregano.
5) Secure the lid and place the pressure valve to "Seal" position.
6) Select "Manual" and cook under "High Pressure" for about 1 minute.
7) Select "Cancel" and carefully do a "Quick" release.
8) Remove the lid and stir in the zucchini and bell pepper.
9) Select "Sauté" and cook for about 5 minutes.
10) Select "Cancel" and discard the bay leaf.
11) Serve hot.

Nutrition Information:
Calories per serving: 318; Carbohydrates: 22.8g; Protein: 19.2g; Fat: 16g; Sugar: 8.4g; Sodium: 1400mg; Fiber: 2.8g

75 – Effortless Veggie Soup

Serves: 6   Cooking Time: 15 minutes   Preparation Time: 15 minutes

Ingredients:

- 3 C. green cabbage, chopped roughly
- 2½ C. vegetable broth
- 1 (14½-oz.) can diced tomatoes
- 3 carrots, peeled and chopped
- 3 celery stalks, chopped
- 1 onion, chopped
- 2 garlic cloves, chopped
- 2 tbsp. apple cider vinegar
- 1 tbsp. fresh lemon juice
- 2 tsp. dried sage

Instructions:

1) In the pot of Instant Pot, place all the ingredients and stir to combine.
2) Secure the lid and place the pressure valve to "Seal" position.
3) Select "Manual" and cook under "High Pressure" for about 15 minutes.
4) Select "Cancel" and do a "Natural" release.
5) Remove the lid and serve hot.

Nutrition Information:

Calories per serving: 62; Carbohydrates: 10.6g; Protein: 3.7g; Fat: 0.8g; Sugar: 5.7g; Sodium: 357mg; Fiber: 3.1g

76 - Bright Green Soup

Serves: 4   Cooking Time: 7 minutes   Preparation Time: 15 minutes

Ingredients:
- 2 tbsp. olive oil
- 1 large celery stalk, chopped
- 1 medium onion, chopped finely
- 1 lb. broccoli, chopped
- 2 medium white potatoes, peeled and cubed
- 2 large garlic cloves, chopped
- 4 C. vegetable broth
- Salt and freshly ground black pepper, to taste
- ½ C. coconut cream
- 1 tbsp. fresh lemon juice

Instructions:

1) Place the oil in Instant Pot and select "Sauté". Then add the celery and onion and cook for about 3-4 minutes.
2) Select "Cancel" and stir in the remaining ingredients except for lemon juice.
3) Secure the lid and place the pressure valve to "Seal" position.
4) Select "Manual" and cook under "High Pressure" for about 3 minutes.
5) Select "Cancel" and do a "Natural" release for about 5 minutes, then do a "Quick" release.
6) Remove the lid and with an immersion blender, blend the soup until smooth.
7) Stir in the coconut cream and lemon juice and serve.

Nutrition Information:
Calories per serving: 294; Carbohydrates: 30.1g; Protein: 11g; Fat: 16.1g; Sugar: 6.2g; Sodium: 856mg; Fiber: 6.9g

77 - Exciting Chickpeas Soup

Serves: 6   Cooking Time: 8 minutes   Preparation Time: 15 minutes

Ingredients:

- 2 tbsp. olive oil
- 1 C. onion, chopped
- 4-5 garlic cloves, crushed
- 1 C. carrot, peeled and chopped
- 1 C. celery stalk, chopped
- 2 (15½ oz.) cans chickpeas, drained and rinsed
- 1 (14½ oz.) can fire-roasted tomatoes
- 2 tbsp. tomato paste
- 1 tbsp. sun-dried tomatoes
- ½ tsp. ground cinnamon
- 2 tsp. ground cumin
- 2 tsp. paprika
- 2 tsp. ground coriander
- Salt and freshly ground black pepper, to taste
- 4 C. vegetable broth
- 2 C. fresh baby spinach, chopped
- 1 tbsp. fresh lemon juice

Instructions:

1) In the pot of Instant Pot, place all the ingredients except for spinach and lemon juice and stir to combine.
2) Secure the lid and place the pressure valve to "Seal" position.
3) Select "Manual" and cook under "High Pressure" for about 8 minutes.
4) Select "Cancel" and do a "Natural" release for about 10 minutes, then do a "Quick" release.
5) Remove the lid and with a potato masher, mash some beans.
6) Stir in the spinach and lemon juice and set aside for about 5 minutes before serving.

Nutrition Information:

Calories per serving: 352; Carbohydrates: 50.5g; Protein: 18.2g; Fat: 9.9g; Sugar: 12.1g; Sodium: 938mg; Fiber: 14g

78 - Comfort Food Soup

Serves: 8   Cooking Time: 30 minutes   Preparation Time: 15 minutes

Ingredients:
- 1 C. yellow split peas
- 1 C. red lentils
- 1 large onion, chopped roughly
- 2 carrots, peeled and chopped roughly
- 5 garlic cloves, chopped
- 1½ tsp. ground cumin
- Salt and freshly ground black pepper, to taste
- 8 C. chicken broth
- 2 tbsp. fresh lemon juice

Instructions:

1) In the pot of Instant Pot, place all the ingredients except for lemon juice and stir to combine.
2) Secure the lid and place the pressure valve to "Seal" position.
3) Select "Manual" and cook under "High Pressure" for about 30 minutes.
4) Select "Cancel" and do a "Natural" release.
5) Remove the lid and stir in lemon juice.
6) Serve hot.

Nutrition Information:
Calories per serving: 226; Carbohydrates: 34.3g; Protein: 17.7g; Fat: 2.1g; Sugar: 4.8g; Sodium: 801mg; Fiber: 14.5g

79 - Turkish Lentil Soup

Serves: 6   Cooking Time: 15 minutes   Preparation Time: 15 minutes

Ingredients:

- 1½ tbsp. olive oil
- 1 medium carrot, peeled and chopped
- 1 medium white onion, chopped
- 1 celery stalk, chopped
- 5 cloves garlic, chopped finely
- 2 C. yellow split peas, rinsed well
- ½ C. canned diced tomatoes
- 1 bay leaf
- 1 tsp. paprika
- 1½ tsp. ground cumin
- ¼ tsp. ground cinnamon
- ¼ tsp. cayenne pepper
- Salt, to taste
- 7 C. vegetable broth
- 1 tbsp. fresh lemon juice
- ½ C. plain Greek yogurt

Instructions:

1) Place the oil in Instant Pot and select "Sauté". Then add the carrot, onion and cook for about 4 minutes.
2) Add the garlic and cook for about 1 minute.
3) Select "Cancel" and stir in the remaining ingredients except for lemon juice and yogurt.
4) Secure the lid and place the pressure valve to "Seal" position.
5) Select "Manual" and cook under "High Pressure" for about 10 minutes.
6) Select "Cancel" and do a "Natural" release for about 10 minutes, then do a "Quick" release.
7) Remove the lid and stir in the lemon juice.
8) Serve with the topping of yogurt.

Nutrition Information:

Calories per serving: 245; Carbohydrates: 35.7g; Protein: 18g; Fat: 5g; Sugar: 7.1g; Sodium: 717mg; Fiber: 13.6g

80 – Satisfying Vegan Soup

Serves: 4   Cooking Time: 12 minutes   Preparation Time: 15 minutes

Ingredients:

- 4 C. vegetable broth
- ½ C. coarse bulgur
- 1 tbsp. olive oil
- 1 yellow onion, chopped
- 4 garlic cloves, minced
- 1 large carrot, peeled and chopped
- 1 tsp. dried oregano
- ½ tsp. dried mint
- ½ tsp. paprika
- ½ tsp. ground cumin
- Salt and freshly ground black pepper, to taste
- 1 (15 oz.) can navy beans, drained and rinsed
- 2 C. fresh baby spinach
- 2 tbsp. fresh lemon juice

Instructions:

1) In the pot of Instant Pot, place all the ingredients except for beans, spinach and lemon juice and stir to combine.
2) Secure the lid and place the pressure valve to "Seal" position.
3) Select "Manual" and cook under "High Pressure" for about 12 minutes.
4) Select "Cancel" and do a "Natural" release for about 10 minutes, then do a "Quick" release.
5) Remove the lid and immediately, stir in the beans, spinach and lemon juice.
6) Immediately, cover the pot with lid for about 5 minutes before serving.

Nutrition Information:

Calories per serving: 308; Carbohydrates: 48.4g; Protein: 17g; Fat: 6.1g; Sugar: 3.5g; Sodium: 900mg; Fiber: 16.1g

81 - Cozy Night Chicken Stew

Serves: 6   Cooking Time: 8 minutes   Preparation Time: 15 minutes

Ingredients:

- 1¼ lb. boneless, skinless chicken thighs
- 4 C. butternut squash, peeled and chopped
- 1 C. yellow onion, chopped
- 2 garlic cloves, chopped
- 1 bay leaf
- 1 tsp. dried oregano
- 1 tsp. ground fennel seeds
- Salt and freshly ground black pepper, to taste
- 4 C. unsalted chicken broth
- ½ C. uncooked quinoa
- 1 oz. olives, pitted and sliced

Instructions:

1) In the pot of Instant Pot, place all the ingredients except for quinoa and olives.
2) Secure the lid and place the pressure valve to "Seal" position.
3) Select "Manual" and cook under "High Pressure" for about 8 minutes.
4) Select "Cancel" and carefully do a "Quick" release.
5) Remove the lid and transfer the chicken thighs onto a cutting board.
6) In the pot, add the quinoa and stir to combine.
7) Select "Sauté" and cook for about 15 minutes, stirring occasionally
8) Shred the chicken thighs and stir into the stew.
9) Select "Cancel" and discard the bay leaf.
10) Serve hot with the topping of olives.

Nutrition Information:

Calories per serving: 315; Carbohydrates: 23.2g; Protein: 33.8g; Fat: 9.4g; Sugar: 3.3g; Sodium: 664mg; Fiber: 3.6g

82 - Sweet & Savory Stew

Serves: 8   Cooking Time: 1 hour   Preparation Time: 15 minutes

Ingredients:

- 3 tbsp. olive oil
- 1½ onions, minced
- 3 lb. beef stew meat, cubed
- 1½ tsp. ground cinnamon
- ¾ tsp. paprika
- ¾ tsp. ground turmeric
- ¼ tsp. ground allspice
- ¼ tsp. ground ginger
- 1½ C. beef broth
- 1½ tbsp. honey
- 1½ C. dried apricots, halved and soaked in hot water until softened and drained
- 1/3 C. almond slivers, toasted

Instructions:

1) Place the oil in Instant Pot and select "Sauté". Then add the onion_and cook for about 3-4 minutes.
2) Stir in the beef and cook for about 3-4 minutes or until browned completely.
3) Stir in the spices and cook for about 2 minutes.
4) Select "Cancel" and stir in the broth and honey.
5) Secure the lid and place the pressure valve to "Seal" position.
6) Select "Meat/Stew" and just use the default time of 50 minutes.
7) Select "Cancel" and do a "Natural" release for about 15 minutes, then do a "Quick" release.
8) Remove the lid and stir in the apricot halves.
9) Serve with the topping of almond slivers.

Nutrition Information:

Calories per serving: 428; Carbohydrates: 10.1g; Protein: 54g; Fat: 18.4g; Sugar: 7.1g; Sodium: 257mg; Fiber: 1.9g

Serves: 6   Cooking Time: 35 minutes   Preparation Time: 15 minutes

Ingredients:

- 1½ lb. beef stew meat, trimmed and cut into 2-inch chunks
- 2 tbsp. olive oil
- 2 medium onions, chopped
- 2 garlic cloves, minced
- ¼ C. tomato paste
- 4 C. beef broth
- 1½ C. dried split peas, rinsed
- 1 (28-oz.) can crushed tomatoes
- 1 tbsp. ground cumin
- ½ tsp. saffron threads, crumbled
- ½ tsp. ground turmeric
- ¼ tsp. ground cinnamon
- ¼ tsp. ground allspice
- Salt and freshly ground black pepper, to taste
- 4 tbsp. fresh lemon juice

Instructions:

1) Season the beef chunks with salt and black pepper evenly.
2) Place the oil in Instant Pot and select "Sauté". Then add the beef chunks in 2 batches and cook for about 4-5 minutes or until browned completely.
3) With a slotted spoon, transfer the beef chunks into a bowl.
4) In the pot, add the onions and garlic and cook for about 2-3 minutes.
5) Add the tomato paste and cook for about 1 minute.
6) Add the broth and cook for about 1 minute, scraping up any browned bits from the bottom.
7) Select "Cancel" and stir in the cooked beef, split peas, tomatoes, spices, salt and black pepper.
8) Secure the lid and place the pressure valve to "Seal" position.
9) Select "Manual" and cook under "High Pressure" for about 25 minutes.
10) Select "Cancel" and do a "Natural" release for about 15 minutes, then do a "Quick" release.
11) Remove the lid and stir in the lemon juice.
12) Serve hot.

Nutrition Information:

Calories per serving: 530; Carbohydrates: 47.7g; Protein: 54.1g; Fat: 13.7g; Sugar: 14.9g; Sodium: 888mg; Fiber: 18.3g

84 – Comfy Meal Stew

Serves: 6   Cooking Time: 1 hour 6 minutes   Preparation Time: 15 minutes

Ingredients:

- ¼ C. flour
- Salt and freshly ground black pepper, to taste
- 2 lb. lamb shoulder, cut into 1-inch cubes
- 2 tbsp. olive oil
- ½ C. celery, chopped
- ½ C. carrots, peeled and chopped
- ½ C. fennel, chopped
- ½ C. leeks, sliced
- 1 tsp. dried rosemary, crushed
- 2 tbsp. brandy
- 1 (28-oz.) can diced tomatoes
- 1 (15-oz.) can chickpeas, drained and rinsed
- 2 C. beef broth
- 1 bay leaf
- 2 tbsp. fresh parsley, chopped

Instructions:

1) In a large shallow bowl, mix together the flour, salt and black pepper.
2) Add the lamb cubes and toss to coat well.
3) Place the oil in Instant Pot and select "Sauté". Then add the lamb cubes in 2 batches and cook for about 4-5 minutes.
4) With a slotted spoon, transfer the lamb cubes into a bowl.
5) In the pot, add the celery, carrots, fennel and cook for about 5 minutes.
6) Stir in the rosemary and brandy and cook for about 1 minute, scraping up any browned bits from the bottom.
7) Select "Cancel" and stir in the cooked lamb cubes, tomatoes, chickpeas, broth and bay leaf.
8) Secure the lid and place the pressure valve to "Seal" position.
9) Select "Manual" and cook under "High Pressure" for about 45 minutes.
10) Select "Cancel" and do a "Natural" release.
11) Remove the lid and serve hot with the garnishing of parsley.

Nutrition Information:

Calories per serving: 478; Carbohydrates: 28.5g; Protein: 49.7g; Fat: 17.4g; Sugar: 4.6g; Sodium: 634mg; Fiber: 5.7g

85 – Toe-Warming Lamb Stew

Serves: 5   Cooking Time: 51 minutes   Preparation Time: 15 minutes

Ingredients:

- 2 lb. lamb shoulder, cubed
- Salt and freshly ground black pepper, to taste
- 1 tbsp. olive oil
- 1 tbsp. butter
- 1 C. onion, chopped
- 2-3 garlic cloves, minced
- 1 tbsp. ginger paste
- 1 tsp. ground coriander
- 1 tsp. ground cinnamon
- ¼-½ C. water
- 8 dried apricots
- 8 dates, pitted
- 2 tbsp. slivered almonds
- 1 tbsp. orange zest
- ½ tbsp. honey
- 1 tsp. ras el hanout

Instructions:

1) Season the lamb cubes with salt and black pepper lightly.
2) Place the oil and butter in Instant Pot and select "Sauté". Then add the lamb cubes in 2 batches and cook for about 4-5 minutes or until browned.
3) With a slotted spoon, transfer the lamb cubes into a bowl.
4) In the pot, add the onion, garlic, ginger paste, coriander and cinnamon and cook for about 4-5 minutes.
5) Add the water and cook for about 1 minute, scraping up any browned bits from the bottom.
6) Select "Cancel" and stir in the lamb cubes.
7) Secure the lid and place the pressure valve to "Seal" position.
8) Select "Manual" and cook under "High Pressure" for about 25 minutes.
9) Select "Cancel" and carefully do a "Natural release."
10) Remove the lid and stir in the remaining ingredients.
11) Select "Sauté" and cook for about 5-10 minutes or until desired thickness of sauce.
12) Select "Cancel" and serve hot.

Nutrition Information:

Calories per serving: 483; Carbohydrates: 22.3g; Protein: 53g; Fat: 20.1g; Sugar: 16.3g; Sodium: 188mg; Fiber:3.

86 - Fragrant Fish Stew

Serves: 4   Cooking Time: 15 minutes   Preparation Time: 15 minutes

Ingredients:

- 4 tbsp. extra-virgin olive oil, divided
- 1 medium red onion, sliced thinly
- 4 garlic cloves, chopped
- ½ C. dry white wine
- ½ lb. red potatoes, cubed
- 1 (15-oz.) can diced tomatoes with juices
- 1/8 tsp. red pepper flakes, crushed
- Salt and freshly ground black pepper, to taste
- 1 (8-oz.) bottled clam juice
- 2½ C. water
- 2 lb. sea bass, cut into 2-inch pieces
- 2 tbsp. fresh dill, chopped
- 2 tbsp. fresh lemon juice

Instructions:

1) Place 2 tbsp. of the oil in Instant Pot and select "Sauté". Then add the onion and cook for about 3 minutes.
2) Add the garlic and cook for about 1 minute.
3) Add the wine and cook for about 1 minute, scraping up any browned bits from the bottom.
4) Select "Cancel" and stir in the potatoes, tomatoes with juices, red pepper flakes, salt, black pepper, clam juice and water.
5) Secure the lid and place the pressure valve to "Seal" position.
6) Select "Manual" and cook under "High Pressure" for about 5 minutes.
7) Select "Cancel" and carefully do a "Quick" release.
8) Remove the lid and select "Sauté".
9) Stir in the fish pieces and cook for about 5 minutes.
10) Select "Cancel" and stir in the dill and lemon juice.
11) Serve hot.

Nutrition Information:
Calories per serving: 533; Carbohydrates: 24.8g; Protein: 56.8g; Fat: 20.4g; Sugar: 6.9g; Sodium: 458mg; Fiber: 3.4g

87 – Winter Dinner Stew

Serves: 6   Cooking Time: 14 minutes   Preparation Time: 20 minutes

Ingredients:

- 3 tbsp. extra-virgin olive oil
- 1 small onion, sliced thinly
- 1 small green bell pepper, seeded and sliced thinly
- 1½ C. tomatoes, chopped
- 2 garlic cloves, minced
- ¼ C. fresh cilantro, chopped and divided
- 2 bay leaves
- 2 tsp. paprika
- Salt and freshly ground black pepper, to taste
- 1 C. fish broth
- 1 lb. shrimp, peeled and deveined
- 12 little neck clams
- 1½ lb. cod fillets, cut into 2-inch chunks

Instructions:

1) Place the oil in Instant Pot and select "Sauté". Then add the onion, bell pepper, tomatoes, garlic, 2 tbsp. of cilantro, bay leaves, paprika, salt and black pepper and cook for about 3-4 minutes.
2) Select "Cancel" and stir in the broth.
3) Submerge the clams and shrimps into the vegetable mixture and top with the cod pieces.
4) Secure the lid and place the pressure valve to "Seal" position.
5) Select "Manual" and cook under "High Pressure" for about 10 minutes.
6) Select "Cancel" and do a "Natural" release for about 10 minutes, then do a "Quick" release.
7) Remove the lid and serve hot with the garnishing of remaining cilantro.

Nutrition Information:
Calories per serving: 450; Carbohydrates: 6.2g; Protein: 79.3g; Fat: 11.9g; Sugar: 2.8g; Sodium: 487mg; Fiber: 1.4g

88 – Palestinian Okra Stew

Serves: 4   Cooking Time: 2minutes   Preparation Time: 15 minutes

Ingredients:

- 1½ lb. fresh okra
- 1 C. onions, chopped
- 1 tbsp. garlic, minced
- 1 (14½-oz.) can diced tomatoes
- 1 tsp. smoked paprika
- ¼ tsp. ground allspice
- Salt, to taste
- ¼ C. vegetable broth
- 2 tbsp. apple cider vinegar
- 2 tbsp. tomato paste
- 1 tbsp. fresh lemon juice

Instructions:

1) In the pot of Instant Pot, place all the ingredients except for tomato paste and lemon juice and stir to combine.
2) Secure the lid and place the pressure valve to "Seal" position.
3) Select "Manual" and cook under "High Pressure" for about 2 minutes.
4) Select "Cancel" and do a "Natural" release for about 5 minutes, then do a "Quick" release.
5) Remove the lid and stir in the tomato paste and lemon juice.
6) Serve hot.

Nutrition Information:

Calories per serving: 114; Carbohydrates: 22.2g; Protein: 5.4g; Fat: 0.8g; Sugar: 7.6g; Sodium: 114mg; Fiber: 7.9g

89 – Meatless-Monday Chickpeas Stew

Serves: 8   Cooking Time: 16 minutes   Preparation Time: 15 minutes

Ingredients:

- ¼ C. olive oil
- 1 onion, chopped
- 7 garlic cloves, chopped finely
- 1 tsp. ground cinnamon
- 1½ tsp. ground cumin
- 2 tsp. sweet paprika
- 1/8 tsp. cayenne pepper
- 3 (14½ oz.) cans chickpeas, rinsed and drained
- 1 (14½ oz.) can diced tomatoes
- 1 C. carrots, peeled and chopped
- 4 C. low-sodium vegetable broth
- Salt and freshly ground black pepper, to taste
- 7 oz. fresh baby spinach

Instructions:

1) Place the oil in Instant Pot and select "Sauté". Then add the onion and cook for about 3-4 minutes.
2) Add the garlic and cook for about 1 minute.
3) Add the spices and cook for about 1 minute.
4) Select "Cancel" and stir in the chickpeas, diced tomatoes with juice, carrots and broth.
5) Secure the lid and place the pressure valve to "Seal" position.
6) Select "Manual" and cook under "High Pressure" for about 10 minutes.
7) Select "Cancel" and do a "Natural" release for about 15 minutes, then do a "Quick" release.
8) Remove the lid and with a potato masher, mash the most of the stew.
9) Add the spinach and stir until wilted.
10) Serve immediately.

Nutrition Information:

Calories per serving: 279; Carbohydrates: 42.5g; Protein: 10.4g; Fat: 8.5g; Sugar: 2.8g; Sodium: 549mg; Fiber: 9g

90 - Super-Quick Stew

Serves: 6   Cooking Time: 4 minutes   Preparation Time: 15 minutes

Ingredients:

- 4 C. cooked pinto beans
- 1 C. frozen corn
- 1 bell pepper, seeded and chopped
- 1 medium onion, chopped
- 1 (14½-oz.) can tomatoes diced with juice
- 1 C. fresh parsley, chopped
- 1 tbsp. red chili powder
- 1½ tsp. ground cumin
- Salt and freshly ground black pepper, to taste
- 1½ C. vegetable broth

Instructions:

1) In the pot of Instant Pot, place all the ingredients and stir to combine.
2) Secure the lid and place the pressure valve to "Seal" position.
3) Select "Manual" and cook under "High Pressure" for about 4 minutes.
4) Select "Cancel" and carefully do a "Quick" release.
5) Remove the lid and serve hot.

Nutrition Information:

Calories per serving: 230; Carbohydrates: 42.4g; Protein: 13.9g; Fat: 2g; Sugar: 5.2g; Sodium: 517mg; Fiber: 13.3g

DESSERT RECIPES

91 – Berry Season Compote

Serves: 8   Cooking Time: 2 minutes   Preparation Time: 10 minutes

Ingredients:
- 4 C. fresh mixed berries (strawberries, raspberries, blueberries and blackberries)
- ¼ C. sugar
- 1 tsp. fresh lemon juice
- 1 tsp. orange juice concentrate

Instructions:

1) In the pot of Instant Pot, place the berries and sugar and with a wooden spoon, stir until sugar is dissolved.
2) Add the lemon juice and orange juice concentrate and stir to combine.
3) Secure the lid and place the pressure valve to "Seal" position.
4) Select "Manual" and cook under "High Pressure" for about 2 minutes.
5) Select "Cancel" and do a "Natural" release for about 10 minutes, then do a "Quick" release.
6) Remove the lid and let the mixture cool before serving.

Nutrition Information:
Calories per serving: 64; Carbohydrates: 14.8g; Protein: 0.5g; Fat: 0.3g; Sugar: 11.3g; Sodium: 0mg; Fiber: 2.5g

92 - Elegant Dessert Pears

Serves: 6   Cooking Time: 13 minutes   Preparation Time: 15 minutes

Ingredients:

- 1 lemon, cut in half
- 3 C. water
- 2 C. white wine
- 2 C. organic cane sugar
- 6 cinnamon sticks
- 6 ripe, but firm pears
- 9 oz. bittersweet chocolate, cut in ½-inch pieces
- ½ C. coconut milk
- ¼ C. coconut oil
- 2 tbsp. maple syrup

Instructions:

1) Select "Sauté" of Instant Pot. Then add the water, wine, sugar and cinnamon sticks and bring to a boil, stirring continuously.
2) Meanwhile, peel the pears, keeping them whole, with the stems intact.
3) Immediately, rub each pear with lemon.
4) Select "Cancel" and squeeze the remaining lemon juice into the sugar syrup.
5) Place the juiced lemon into the syrup. Now, place the pears into the hot syrup.
6) Secure the lid and place the pressure valve to "Seal" position. Select "Manual" and cook under "High Pressure" for about 3 minutes.
7) Select "Cancel" and carefully do a "Quick" release.
8) Remove the lid and with a slotted spoon, transfer the pears onto a platter.
9) Let the syrup cool slightly.
10) Place the cooled syrup over pears.
11) For chocolate sauce: place the chocolate in a bowl. Set aside.
12) In a small saucepan, place the coconut milk, coconut oil and maple syrup over medium heat and bring to a gentle simmer.
13) Remove from the heat and immediately, pour the milk mixture over the chocolate. Let it sit for about 1 minute.
14) With a wire whisk, beat until smooth. Pour the warm sauce over the pears and serve.

Nutrition Information:

Calories per serving: 712; Carbohydrates: 126.5g; Protein: 2.7g; Fat: 18.4g; Sugar: 45.5g; Sodium: 49mg; Fiber: 7g

93 - Apple Juice Poached Pears

Serves: 4   Cooking Time: 6 minutes   Preparation Time: 10 minutes

Ingredients:

- 4 firm pears
- 4 C. unsweetened apple juice
- 1 C. frozen blackberries
- 2 cinnamon sticks
- 2 star anise
- 5 cardamom pods
- 2 tsp. vanilla extract

Instructions:

1) Peel pears and cut bottoms of pears, so they sit flat.
2) In the pot of Instant Pot, arrange the pears, stem up and top with apple juice.
3) Submerge the blackberries, whole spices and vanilla extract into the juice.
4) Secure the lid and place the pressure valve to "Seal" position.
5) Select "Manual" and cook under "High Pressure" for about 6 minutes.
6) Select "Cancel" and carefully do a "Quick" release.
7) Remove the lid and with a slotted spoon, transfer the pears onto a platter.
8) Through a fine mesh strainer, strain the juice,
9) Pour the juice over pears and serve.

Nutrition Information:

Calories per serving: 259; Carbohydrates: 64.5g; Protein: 1.4g; Fat: 0.7g; Sugar: 9.4g; Sodium: 11mg; Fiber: 8.6g

94 – Chocolate Lover's Cake

Serve: 1   Cooking Time: 10 minutes   Preparation Time: 15 minutes

Ingredients:

- 4 tbsp. all-purpose flour
- 4 tbsp. sugar
- 1 tbsp. cocoa powder
- ¼ tsp. orange zest, grated
- Pinch of salt
- ½ tsp. baking powder
- 1 medium egg
- 4 tbsp. milk
- 2 tbsp. extra-virgin olive oil

Instructions:

1) In a bowl, add all ingredients and beat vigorously until well combined.
2) Place the mixture into a lightly greased mug.
3) Arrange the trivet in the bottom of Instant Pot and pour 1 cup of water.
4) Place the mug on top of the trivet.
5) Secure the lid and place the pressure valve to "Seal" position.
6) Select "Manual" and cook under "High Pressure" for about 10 minutes.
7) Select "Cancel" and carefully do a "Quick" release.
8) Remove the lid and serve immediately.

Nutrition Information:

Calories per serving: 642; Carbohydrates: 79.50g; Protein: 11.8g; Fat: 34.7g; Sugar: 1.3g; Sodium: 249mg; Fiber: 2.6g

95 – Moist Date Cake

Serves: 16   Cooking Time: 40 minutes   Preparation Time: 20 minutes

Ingredients:

- 1½ C. seedless dates, chopped
- 1½ C. water
- 1 tsp. baking soda
- 2 large eggs
- ¾ C. sugar
- ½ C. unsalted butter, softened
- 1 tsp. vanilla extract
- 1½ C. all-purpose flour
- ¼ tsp. salt
- 2 tsp. baking powder
- 1 tsp. instant coffee granules
- 1 tsp. unsweetened cocoa powder

Instructions:

1) Select "Sauté" of Instant Pot and adjust it to the "More" mode. Then add 1½ C. of water and bring to a boil. Add the dates and cook for about 5 minutes.
2) Stir in the baking soda and select "Cancel". Carefully remove the steel insert from the Instant Pot and set aside for 15 minutes.
3) In a blender, add the eggs, sugar, butter and vanilla extract and pulse until well combined.
4) Add the date mixture and mix until well combined. Add the remaining ingredients and pulse until just combined.
5) Place the mixture into a greased 6-inch Bundt cake pan evenly.
6) With a piece of foil, cover the pan. Arrange the trivet in the bottom of Instant Pot and pour 1 C. of water.
7) Place the cake pan on top of the trivet.
8) Secure the lid and place the pressure valve to "Seal" position.
9) Select "Manual" and cook under "High Pressure" for about 30 minutes.
10) Select "Cancel" and do a "Natural" release for about 15 minutes, then do a "Quick" release.
11) Remove the lid and carefully, transfer the Bundt pan onto a wire rack.
12) Uncover the pan and let it cool for about 10 minutes.
13) Carefully invert the cake onto the wire rack to cool completely before serving.
14) Cut the cake into desired sized slices and serve.

Nutrition Information:

Calories per serving: 186; Carbohydrates: 31.3g; Protein: 2.5g; Fat: 6.6g; Sugar: 20.1g; Sodium: 166mg; Fiber: 1.7g

96 - Delicious Coffee-Time Cake

Serves: 8   Cooking Time: 35 minutes   Preparation Time: 15 minutes

Ingredients:

- 2 C. all-purpose flour
- 1 tsp. baking soda
- 1 tsp. baking powder
- ¼ tsp. salt
- 1 large egg
- 1 C. plain unsweetened Greek yogurt
- 1 C. granulated sugar
- ½ C. unsalted butter, softened
- 3 tbsp. fresh lemon juice, divided
- 1 tbsp. lemon zest, grated
- 1 C. confectioner's sugar
- 1 tbsp. half-and-half

Instructions:

1) In a bowl, mix together the flour, baking soda, baking powder and salt.
2) In another bowl, add the egg, yogurt, granulated sugar, butter, 2 tbsp. of lemon juice and lemon zest and with a hand mixer, beat until smooth.
3) Add the flour mixture and with the hand mixer, mix until well combined.
4) Place the mixture onto a greased 6-C. Bundt pan evenly.
5) Arrange a paper towel over the top of pan, then cover the paper towel and pan with a piece of foil loosely.
6) Arrange the trivet in the bottom of Instant Pot and pour 1 C. of water. Place the cake pan on top of the trivet.
7) Secure the lid and place the pressure valve to "Seal" position.
8) Select "Manual" and cook under "High Pressure" for about 35 minutes.
9) Select "Cancel" and do a "Natural" release.
10) Remove the lid and carefully, transfer the Bundt pan onto a wire rack. Uncover the pan and let it cool for about 10 minutes.
11) Carefully invert the cake onto the wire rack to cool completely before glazing.
12) For glaze: in a bowl, add the confectioners' sugar, half-and-half and remaining lemon juice and beat until smooth.
13) Spread the glaze over cake and serve.

Nutrition Information:

Calories per serving: 403; Carbohydrates: 66.7g; Protein: 6g; Fat: 13.1g; Sugar: 42.2g; Sodium: 348mg; Fiber: 0.9g

97 - Delightful Cream Cake

Serves: 12   Cooking Time: 35 minutes   Preparation Time: 15 minutes

Ingredients:

For Cake:
- 1 C. sour cream
- 1 tsp. baking soda
- 1 C. butter
- 2 C. Swerve confectioners
- 5 eggs

- 2½ C. blanched almond flour
- 1 C. unsweetened flaked coconut
- 1 tsp. baking powder
- 2 tsp. vanilla extract

For Frosting:
- 8 oz. cream cheese, softened
- ½ C. butter, softened
- 1 tsp. vanilla extract
- 2 C. Swerve confectioners

- 2 tbsp. heavy cream
- ½ C. walnuts, chopped
- 1 C. unsweetened flaked coconut

Instructions:

1) Line the bottom of a greased 7-inch round spring-form cake pan with greased parchment paper. Set aside. For cake: in a small bowl, add the sour cream and baking soda and mix well. Set aside.
2) In a large bowl, add butter and sweetener and beat until light and fluffy.
3) Add the remaining ingredients and mix until just combined. Place the mixture into the prepared cake pan evenly.
4) Arrange the trivet in the bottom of Instant Pot and pour 1 C. of water.
5) Place the cake pan on top of the trivet.
6) Secure the lid and place the pressure valve to "Seal" position. Select "Manual" and cook under "High Pressure" for about 35 minutes.
7) Select "Cancel" and do a "Natural" release for about 20 minutes, then do a "Quick" release.
8) Remove the lid and carefully, transfer the Bundt pan onto a wire rack to cool for about 10 minutes.
9) Carefully invert the cake onto the wire rack to cool completely before frosting.
10) For frosting: in a medium bowl, add all ingredients except for walnuts and flaked coconut and beat until light and fluffy.
11) Fold in the walnuts and flaked coconut.
12) Spread the frosting over cake and serve.

Nutrition Information:
Calories per serving: 579; Carbohydrates: 9.2g; Protein: 6.3g; Fat: 56.4g; Sugar: 2g; Sodium: 363mg; Fiber: 4.1g

98 - Zesty Cheesecake

Serves: 6   Cooking Time: 35 minutes   Preparation Time: 15 minutes

Ingredients:
- 1½ C. graham crackers, crushed
- 2 tbsp. unsalted butter, melted
- Pinch kosher salt
- 1¼ C. whole milk ricotta cheese
- ½ C. mascarpone cheese, softened
- 3 large eggs
- ½ C. granulated sugar
- 2 tbsp. all-purpose flour
- 2 tsp. lemon zest, grated
- 1 tsp. fresh lemon juice
- 1 tsp. vanilla extract
- ½ C. lemon curd

Instructions:

1) Line the bottom of a greased 7-inch round springform pan with a parchment paper.
2) In a food processor, add the graham crackers, butter and salt and pulse until mixture resembles coarse sand.
3) Place the crumb mixture into prepared pan and, press into an even layer onto the bottom and ½-inch up the sides of pan.
4) Freeze the pan until firm. In a food processor, add ricotta cheese, mascarpone cheese, eggs, sugar, flour, lemon zest, lemon juice and vanilla extract and pulse until smooth.
5) Place the filling over the prepared crust. Arrange a paper towel over the top of pan, then cover the paper towel and pan with a piece of foil loosely.
6) Arrange the trivet in the bottom of Instant Pot and pour 1 C. of water.
7) Place the cake pan on top of the trivet.
8) Secure the lid and place the pressure valve to "Seal" position.
9) Select "Manual" and cook under "High Pressure" for about 35 minutes.
10) Select "Cancel" and do a "Natural" release.
11) Remove the lid and carefully, transfer the cake pan onto a wire rack.
12) Uncover the pan and let it cool for about 45-60 minutes.
13) Cover the pan and refrigerate for at least 4 hours or overnight, before serving.
14) Spread lemon curd over cheesecake and serve.

Nutrition Information:
Calories per serving: 420; Carbohydrates: 43.8g; Protein: 54.7g; Fat: 23.3g; Sugar: 29.1g; Sodium: 365mg; Fiber: 0.7g

99 – Greek Wedding Cheesecake

Serves: 8   Cooking Time: 28 minutes   Preparation Time: 15 minutes

Ingredients:

For Crust:
- ¾ C. wafer-cookie crumbs
- 3 tbsp. butter, melted
- 1 tbsp. sugar
- ½ tsp. almond extract

For Filling:
- 2 (8-oz.) packages cream cheese
- 1 C. sugar
- 2 eggs
- 3 tbsp. whipping cream
- ¼ C. amaretto
- ¼ C. plus 1 tbsp. cocoa powder
- ¼ C. all-purpose flour
- 1 tsp. vanilla extract
- 1/3 C. semi-sweet chocolate chips

Instructions:

1) For crust: in a food processor, add all the ingredients and pulse until mixture resembles coarse sand.
2) Place the crumb mixture into a greased 7-inch springform pan and, press into an even layer onto the bottom and ½-inch up the sides of pan.
3) For filling: in a bowl, add the cream cheese and sugar and beat until smooth.
4) Add the eggs and whipping cream and beat until well combined.
5) Add the amaretto, cocoa powder, flour and vanilla extract and beat for about 1 more minute.
6) Fold in the chocolate chips. Place the filling over the prepared crust.
7) Arrange the trivet in the bottom of Instant Pot and pour 1 C. of water.
8) Place the cake pan on top of the trivet.
9) Secure the lid and place the pressure valve to "Seal" position. Select "Manual" and cook under "High Pressure" for about 28 minutes.
10) Select "Cancel" and do a "Natural" release.
11) Remove the lid and carefully, transfer the cake pan onto a wire rack to cool for about 45-55 minutes.
12) Cover the pan and refrigerate for at least 4 hours, or overnight, before serving.

Nutrition Information:
Calories per serving: 494; Carbohydrates: 44.4g; Protein: 8g; Fat: 30.9g; Sugar: 39.1g; Sodium: 849mg; Fiber: 1.3g

100 – Sweet-Tooth Carving Tiramisu Cheesecake

Serves: 8   Cooking Time: 55 minutes   Preparation Time: 20 minutes

Ingredients:

For Crust:
- 1½ C. ladyfingers, crushed finely
- 1½ C. chocolate graham cracker crumbs
- 1 tsp. instant espresso powder
- 6 tbsp. butter, melted

For Filling:
- 16 oz. cream cheese, softened
- 8 oz. mascarpone cheese, softened
- ¾ C. granulated sugar
- 2 large eggs
- 2 tbsp. powdered sugar
- 1 tbsp. instant espresso powder
- 4 tbsp. coffee liqueur, divided
- 1 tsp. vanilla extract
- 6-8 ladyfingers, halved

For Icing:
- 8 oz. mascarpone cheese, softened
- 4 oz. cream cheese, softened
- 8 oz. butter, softened
- 1 tbsp. espresso powder
- 1 tbsp. coffee liqueur
- 3 C. powdered sugar

For Sprinkling:
- 2 tbsp. cocoa powder

Instructions:

1) Line the bottom of a greased 8-inch round springform pan with a parchment paper. For crust: in a bowl, add all ingredients and mix until mixture resembles coarse sand.
2) Place the crumb mixture into the prepared springform pan and, press into an even layer onto the bottom and ½-inch up the sides of pan. Freeze the pan until set.
3) In the bowl of a stand mixer, add the cream cheese, mascarpone and granulated sugar and beat until light and fluffy. Add eggs, powdered sugar, 2 tbsp. coffee liqueur espresso powder and mix until smooth.
4) Place half of the filling mixture over crust. Arrange ladyfingers halves on top of filling. Brush the tops of ladyfingers with the remaining coffee liqueur.
5) Now, place the remaining filling mixture on top of ladyfingers. With a foil cover the pan. With a fork, poke small hole in top of foil to allow steam to escape.
6) Arrange the trivet in the bottom of Instant Pot and pour 1 C. of water. Place the cake pan on top of the trivet. Secure the lid and place the pressure valve to "Seal" position.
7) Select "Manual" and cook under "High Pressure" for about 55 minutes.
8) Select "Cancel" and carefully do a "Natural" release for about 10 minutes, then do a "Quick" release.
9) Remove the lid and carefully, transfer the cake pan onto a wire rack. Uncover the pan and let it cool for about 45-60 minutes.
10) For icing: in large bowl, add cream cheese, mascarpone and butter and beat until light and fluffy. Add coffee liqueur and espresso powder and mix until well combined. Slowly, add powdered sugar and mix until smooth.
11) Spread icing over the cheesecake and sprinkle with cocoa powder. Refrigerate to chill before serving.

Nutrition Information: Calories per serving: 1011; Carbohydrates: 96.6g; Protein: 54.7g; Fat: 62.8g; Sugar: 71.4g; Sodium: 636mg; Fiber: 1.6g

CONCLUSION

The Mediterranean diet is often considered one of the healthiest lifestyle choices to be made. By switching to a diet that has a primary focus on plant-based foods, people experience a large number of health benefits. Heart health improves, weight management becomes easier, and there may even be a lower risk of cancer.

Combined with the use of a pressure cooker, the Mediterranean diet may become a convenience in your home. There are thousands of Mediterranean recipes that use a pressure cooker. The combination gives you access to more nutrients, improves the absorption of important chemicals in the food you eat, and ultimately provides for faster meal times.